Buster Brown's America:
Recollections, Reveries, Reflections

Incorporating *This Old Writer: A Journal of a Plague Year.*

Buster Brown's America:
Recollections, Reveries, Reflections

Incorporating *This Old Writer: A Journal of a Plague Year.*

Igor Webb

ODD VOLUMES

of
The Fortnightly Review

CHAVAGNES-EN-PAILLERS

2022

ODD VOLUMES
The Fortnightly Review
96 rue du Calvaire
85250 Chavagnes-en-Paillers
France.

ISBN 978-0-9997058-0-3

Published for subscribers.

info@fortnightlyreview.co.uk

Acknowledgments

I would like to thank the editors of the following magazines, where some the writing in this book first appeared, usually in slightly different form: *The American Scholar*, where "Buster Brown's America" first appeared; *The Hudson Review*, where "Horatio Hornblower" first appeared; *Partisan Review*, where my review essay on Philip Roth's *The Human Stain* first appeared (it was reprinted in Harold Bloom's Modern Critical Views collection *Philip Roth* (2003); and *The Fortnightly Review*, where "Now," "On Longinus and bread...and the sublime" and "Matthias' Laments" first appeared. I am especially grateful to Robert and Elizabeth Murphy of Dos Madres Press, which included "Buster Brown's America" in my book *Christopher Smart's Cat* (2018).

My essay on Philip Roth's *Nemesis* was presented as part of the panel discussion at "Philip Roth's *Nemesis:* An Evening at YIVO," May 18, 2011.

Table of Contents

WHAT TO CALL IT:
A Protest Against Genre

The scholar-critics of his day sniped at Montaigne's writing. He was demeaning the high style of philosophy, as they saw it, by his digressions and anecdotes and especially by his intrusion of tawdry details about himself into argument. "I am myself the matter of my book" was not what they wanted to hear.

But it is what makes Montaigne great. "He was the first," as William Hazlitt memorably put it, "to say as an author what he felt as a man."

The "essays" Montaigne and Hazlitt wrote were always about the writers as much as their subjects, or about their subjects as seen in the full light of the person of the writer, and both Montaigne and Hazlitt followed the trail of their ideas and impressions without a second thought about whether they were violating the rules of genre.

Ironically, today, Montaigne's and Hazlitt's heirs, the writers of cross-genre and hybrid work, of "creative nonfiction," have inadvertently cast a very wet blanket over what has come to be known as Montaigne's creation, the essay. The essay is what you write when you're not being creative. Most high school classrooms in this country teach their students not to use "I" in an essay. If your book gets labelled "essays" you can be pretty sure only close family and friends will bother to crack it open.

This is a protest, then, against genre.

The consciousness trying to make sense of things, the writer, as in their own way both Virginia Woolf and Milan Kundera (among others! and we don't have to go back to Montaigne) have taken pains to tell everybody, the consciousness trying to make sense of things is bombarded by sensations (Woolf) and also thoughts, ideas, memories (Kundera), and it's a form of intellectual imprisonment to force the writer to censor and edit out the sensations and intrusive thoughts for the sake of a system of categorization, that is, genre with its rules, borders, permissions and prohibitions.

You're not supposed to use "I" in an essay just as you're not supposed to introduce the writer, the person who holds the pen and needs a haircut, into the fictional narrative.

But even Tolstoy bristled at the demand that he call *War and Peace* something, such as a novel. He insisted it is not a novel, it is simply *War and Peace*. He loved all those passages on the philosophy of history, true, but for him the book is of one piece: he couldn't disentangle the narrative from his reflections on history and fate; he couldn't disentangle how things happen to the czar or to that corpulent little man with a cold commanding his armies at Austerlitz and how things happen to (the also corpulent) Pierre; and needless to say as a Russian aristocrat he was not thinking of the people who have to sell the book and need to know whether it's to be set on the shelf with novels or cookbooks . . . and he was disdainful of the ones who have to review it.

So what should we call it? In his most recent book, *A Primer for Forgetting* (2019), Lewis Hyde begins with a brief introduction, titled "What This Is" to explain that "the citations, aphorisms, anecdotes, stories, and reflections" of his book are the result of his decision to abandon expository prose for . . . what this new book is. "What a relief," he says, "to make a book whose free associations are happily foregrounded, a book that does not so much argue its point of departure as more simply sketch the territory . . ." And Hyde is hardly alone. On the contrary, his book can be set alongside Maggie Nelson's *Argonauts* and Eula Biss' *Having and Being Had* and Claudia Rankine's *Citizen* and so many other works the publishers don't know how to classify, books that aim to get at what's true through an uncensored act of imagination, and as every reader in his library nook and every writer gripping her notepad knows acts of imagination don't always behave according to the rules of generic manners (citations, aphorisms, anecdotes, stories, and reflections).

So I don't know what I should call the writing you will find here, but I do know it includes citations, aphorisms, anecdotes, stories, recollections, reveries, reflections . . .

I

Setting Out

BUSTER BROWN'S
AMERICA

On 207th street way uptown in Manhattan, a couple of blocks north of the elevated subway, there used to be a Buster Brown shoe store. This was in the 1950s. The most wonderful thing in that store was not a shoe but rather a magical contraption kept in the rear against the back wall, a tall wooden box resembling an elongated cardboard carton or a miniature coffin. At its base this tall box had an opening into which you stuck your feet, strangely stiff in their not-yet-purchased new shoes; at the top the box was enclosed and there protruded a rectangular viewer through which you looked down at—this was the magical part—something like an X-ray of your feet darkly outlined in their casing of new shoes! It was a kind of out-of-body experience before I knew there were such things, and blessed by science: a scientific measure to ensure that your brand-new shoes fit perfectly.

I loved, feared, and felt altogether ga-ga about that elongated contraption. It was the weirdest object of study among the welter of things that I, having just got off the boat, wanted so badly to see and feel and value the way any American kid would. Who knows how this should have been done: I experienced it as being akin to what's expected of a devotee. The objects of my devotion included Campbell's baked beans, Superman, Roy Rogers, capguns, baseball gloves, Spalding balls, the Shadow, Bazooka gum, peanut butter, Coke, Chevys, Louis Armstrong, Dinah Shore, Milton Berle, Jerry Lewis, Sid Caesar, Imogen Coca, the Pledge of Allegiance (at that very moment still godless but about to become a pious weapon in the war against godless Communism) . . . Anyway, you get the point. I was ardently devoted to mastering all this so I could claim my destiny as an American boy.

Curiously, if you looked the wrong way, the back of the Buster Brown store appeared distinctly shabby—you could see down to the storage area, which didn't have a carpet on the floor; there were little bits of crepe paper and tags and such lying around; and dust. I liked that, for all that it made uneasy—I mean the almost kinky consanguinity of the brilliance of the latest thing, all lit up, as it were, and the tawdry back of the store. And one more thing, to do with language and the important mysteries of advertising. Even then, when my American English was an unreliable, uncertain, crude instrument for the apprehension of things, even then I wondered about the prudence of naming a store something as hoky as "Buster Brown." There was a boy attached to this name, a boy after whom the store was named. The ads about this boy confused me—I was never quite clear about where the boy was supposed to be from, and what sort of life he was supposed to be living. But it seemed clear even to me as a just-landed immigrant that he was of the wrong time and the wrong place, of a simpler time and a more rural place, and hence either an archaic or a nostalgic figure, and it puzzled me how one or the other could be very good for business.

We arrived in New York by boat. We got off the boat and were driven to the apartment in the east thirties of a landsman, where the adults gathered around the dinette to catch up on their news and I—I was ten years old--was plopped in front of the tv. I had never seen such a thing before. It was the afternoon. On the screen was a show from a zoo, maybe the Bronx Zoo, a show about snakes. A man in an open-necked white shirt stood next to a not-very-large glass case, and in this case a black snake moved extremely slowly, sometimes across the glass, sometimes across the screen. This all of course happened in black and white, so in truth I don't know what color shirt the man wore or what color the snake was. Black and white. For the most part the snake barely moved; and there were long silences. Nevertheless I was transfixed. My first day in New York, in the United States of America.

We finally settled way uptown, in Inwood. Inwood in those days—maybe that's what accounts for the Buster Brown shoe store—was a neighborhood of the respectable poor. It was appallingly clean, especially once you got to the side streets. These were especially clean, long rows of wide sidewalks and tenements, mainly in bland, dusty pale brick. Inside these apartment houses the hallways were long and ill-lit. But there was not much to distinguish the inside from the outside: both were hugely empty, a neat, vacant streetscape, without money. No one had enough to get anything dirty, never mind to litter. These just were the streets of respectable poverty—a poverty, incidentally, that achieved the American ideal: a true Melting Pot of poverty without blatant ethnic or racial distinction. Jews, Irish, other eastern Europeans, African-Americans .

. we were all more or less the same. Our upstanding isolation on the periphery of American affluence at a moment of such total conviction in the *rightness* of things American, such as split-level houses and G.E. refrigerators—our poverty rendered us if not altogether equal then companionable. In the distance, bright lights, big city.

The houses to the West of Broadway, from Broadway to edge of Inwood Park, these were the domain of the better off. (Appropriately, you had to walk uphill all the way from my house down by the Harlem River to this stretch of modest privilege perched above the Hudson.) All my Jewish friends who were old American, in other words, who had been born in the country, lived up there. The Catholic church up the street from my primary school—P. S. 98 Manhattan—sat on the West side of Broadway too: the Good Shepherd Church. I owe something crucial to that church, to which I was also, for a time, devoted. It was at the Good Shepherd Church that I fell from grace, and in this utterly reliable way became an American boy.

Here's what I mean: My mother had decided that, now I was to be an American—having arrived in New York City we were never again, my mother concluded, going to pack up and migrate—so, now that I was to be an American, I would of course have to cease being not only a Slovak, but a Jew. I would become an all-American Catholic boy. She didn't know that all-American boys are not Catholic. In our hometown in Slovakia, on one side of the town square stood the synagogue, on the other, the Catholic church. That was it, the two possibilities. I don't think she altogether understood about Protestantism, or had much notion of the lineage of American power. But maybe I am wrong. Maybe she couldn't quite bring herself to go that far, to aspire to slipping into ranks so wholly alien, to be so daring . . .

In any event I was packed off to the Good Shepherd Church for religious instruction, the only boy in my group studying at once for first communion and confirmation, since at the age when I ought to have first rendered my confession and knelt at the altar and received the body and blood of Jesus Christ I was stranded in what for my family was the no-man's-land at the foot of the Andes mountains in Ecuador, where, incongruously, we had landed after the Holocaust. I am not going to say much about why we arrived there, of all unlikely places. The fact is there really weren't many places to go; we couldn't get in to the U.S.; and one of my mother's brothers was already living in Quito, the Ecuadorean capital. Still, it was a mistake. Whatever it might have meant actually to blend into the Ecuadorean streets, to speak Latin American Spanish, to belong *there* . . . all of this never quite rose to the level of something plausible and real. Rather Ecuador was simply a no-man's-land--in the sense that my parents felt out of place there immediately and always, could not imagine how to set roots there, and had no sooner arrived there than they laid plans to leave (although this took another five years). We were therefore neither one thing nor another—not Ecuadoreans, not Europeans; not Catholics, not Jews . . . and so forth. Whatever I was, as a five-year-old boy in Quito, that boy vanished, lost between possibilities. When I arrived in New York I was determined not to have any such thing happen again. I was going to be someone once more.

This took a lot of doing, and didn't work out according to plan. My mother's plan was to get me wiped even more clean of the stain of identities than I had been in the radical indeterminacy of our Ecuadorean exile, as if I could be wiped clean of all and every association with anything for which there might exist an exclusive name, such as a nation or a race and especially of anything that might betray me as singed by the Holocaust. Only in my invisibility would safety lie. The first step in this Houdini act was to be performed at the altar of the Good Shepherd Church.

Almost half a century later my father is serving dinner to my Israeli second cousin's grandfather, on her mother's side. (Have you followed that? One of my father's brothers escaped the Nazis across Romania to Palestine, married, had two daughters— and was killed in the 1947 war. One of these daughters, Avigail, herself had two daughters, one of whom, Judy, works for El-Al and regularly visits my father, now the patriarch of the family across several continents. On this visit she comes with her mother's father, an old Zionist, one of the founding Israeli generation.) The two old men, my father and Judy's grandfather, get on like a house on fire. They find they have everything in common. They eat and wave their hands to rouse up the past. Among the things they have most in common is an upbringing of sturdy or better pugilistic anti-clericalism, a kind of peasant suspiciousness of religion. "We were poor. Everyone was poor. I did not believe it when they told me God would help me. Nobody helped me," my father says. Ari—Judy's grandfather—adds with a note of delight and fury, "That's it! You think I was different? When the Hassidim came by our house we threw stones at them!" My father jumps up. "I threw stones at them. I hated them!"

My parents came from a culture of emphatic secularism of a kind that no one would tolerate today in the United States. For one thing it would be seen as disrespectful, our only remaining word for sin. But to my parents and to so many Jews of their time and place religion meant, more than anything, the commitment to backwardness. Everything progressive, everything modern, everything promising hope and better things was for them not simply a-religious but anti-religious. They threw stones at the Hassidim!

Consequently at the time I was enrolled for instruction in the Good Shepherd Church I had had no experience of church, synagogue, or of anything having to do with religion, either as concept, or ritual, or place. I must have known what the designation "a place of worship" means. But these words meant nothing to me, in reality. They referred to some abstract thing of which I had no experience. When I first entered the Good Shepherd Church, with its vaulting ceiling, its dark air spiced with incense and candle-smoke, its blatant figures of holy agony, its grotesque bleeding hearts—I reeled, felt nauseous, and—truly—almost fainted. I felt a kind of blissful sickness made of equal parts rapture and terror.

This is where things began to go wrong—for my mother, and for me. My mother—then as always—took it as axiomatic that I saw the world as she saw the world. It would be a good thing to become a titular Catholic. It would provide a way to pass, a key to the kingdom, a cloak of invisibility. But I was a serious boy impelled by all of my experience of wandering and breathtaking escapes toward communities of belonging, and by all the amorality of dispossession, toward moral achievement. My poor mother was flabbergasted to find me a prostrate penitent ambitious for salvation. I began regular attendance at services; I confessed and prayed; I was overcome with unworthiness and hope. I was going to be good.

The mass in those days was still conducted in Latin, which served my purposes exactly. The mystery at the heart of the faith was inscrutable, inaccessible, unintelligible—but melodious, authoritative, commanding, beautiful, disciplined, powerful beyond reason or understanding. It was the sort of thing I am sure every child—diminutive in a great world—finds completely convincing. God knows; God Is; before Him how small and transparent we are, how pitifully guilty. At the same time, here was something to aspire to, a glory beyond calculation, beyond everyday grubbing, something awesome in the old sense of the word—something vast and in its vastness equal to the ravenous passions of childhood.

I became at once an abject pilgrim in the Christian epic—I was going to be good, to be saved, to be elected to the community of eternal privilege. My parents were stunned and appalled.

I need a digression here. Our apartment was on the third floor (the top floor) of a new, block-long building set back from the street and fronted by what were called "gardens." These gardens were no more than a patch of lawn with a couple of trees here and there but still no other buildings in the neighborhood could claim any such sylvan accessories. Never mind that what I saw directly in front of my bedroom window was a garage for Pabst Blue Ribbon beer delivery trucks: ours were "garden apartments," practically suburban. On the street level this block of apartments was divided into several sections, each with a separate entrance but below ground the basement was one continuous cavern, with rooms for storage and whatnot, a long stretch with the massive boilers, and at the end farthest from where I lived the apartment of the super, Mr. Kotlowitz. Mr. Kotlowitz had one child, a son two or three years older than I, named Billy. For some reason there were few children living in our garden apartments—aside from me there were Esther Blank, a year older, stately, the object of my adoration and fantasy, to whom I never said more than three words; Tommy Murphy, a classmate, whose father owned a candy store on 207th street (he made great egg sodas); and Billy.

The basement was Billy's kingdom, and served us—that is, the boys—as our private amusement park. It was perfect—there was never anyone else around; there were nooks and crannies, machinery, odd bits of equipment, stray tools . . . Billy, as the eldest and biggest of us, ruled. He liked to horse around, to grab you and heave you to the ground, or onto the creaky bed that stood incongruously in one of the otherwise empty rooms and where we would wrestle and punch each other. In that room too Billy kept his set of pornographic pictures. The basement was hot. We would be flushed from having tossed each other around. It was as if Billy's pornographic pictures were a little bit of purgatory. These were crude black-and-white photos of naked women in various explicit but unseductive poses—women on their backs with their legs wide apart, revealing a dark, unruly center; women on all fours photographed from behind; women holding their breasts up to the camera in their palms, and so forth. Billy would pass these out one by one, and Tommy and I would adopt a swaggering nonchalance to hide our fascination and fright.

Now there are some things in the house-of-horrors of early adolescence, where so much experience is creepily distorted, that you just can't admit you haven't mastered. At an age when no one knew anything at all about sex it is astonishing how we all pretended to dulled familiarity with each fragment of carnal knowledge. Like James Joyce's boys in *Dubliners*, we too, comprehensively short on experience and self-knowledge, found our daring extended only to pulling down the shades and peeping out in a fever of adoration and shame. Everything about our unruly bodies stained the daily world; we laughed hysterically, blushed and leered, lived two lives, one undemonstrative and common, one secret, overheated, shameful.

In woodworking class at my junior high, the boldest of us, Tony Russo, broke the ice by claiming intimacies I—and probably most everyone else— found dizzying and baffling. Not the smartest kid in the class, he had finally found something to give him an edge, an actual intellectual advantage, over the rest of us, and seemed to have mastered an anatomical vocabulary of breadth, precision, and a kind of vulgar pedantry. Pretty soon the whole bunch of us were throwing around whispered queries. In the end even Tony had to admit there *were* things he couldn't be quite sure of. It was decided that some one of us, palpably respectable and decent, an obviously good boy of whom no bad thoughts could be entertained—some one of us like that should go to his doctor and ask. I was selected.

Our family doctor, Dr. Kranz, was a thin, gray, kindly old man, maybe in his sixties, and also a Slovak Jew. Occasionally my parents saw him socially. It was unthinkable that I could ask him how many times a day would be safe to jerk off—one of my friends' questions—not to mention what words I could possibly use to fulfill my delicate assignment (my vocabulary was no match for Tony Russo's). But then, was there anyone at all to go to? This was before the days of sex education or of lucid discussion about sex with your parents (assuming there really is such a thing); and this wasn't a subject you could talk to God about.

For my mother my introduction to the Good Shepherd Church backfired when against all expectations I got religion. For me, the obligations of faith brought me soon enough to the simplest moral crisis, the one in which flesh and spirit clash. As a boy, as a good Catholic boy, I did not know that my pain and struggle were a cliché. Images from Billy's card collection, Esther Blank's haunches as she walked in front of me to school, the bra ads in my mother's *Vogue*—it seemed as if everything conspired to taint my waking and dreaming with sin.

I could not find a way out. I could not find anyone to speak to. I could not confess. It was no more thinkable to put my sin into words, say in the confessional, than it was likely I would never sin again. In fact I had just done so, was about to do so, would have liked to have done so, was thinking of doing so, was thinking of little else. Even assuming I could have found a way to speak in the confessional, how could I ever have made it safely through to the next morning's communion?

In this way the days lengthened to weeks. I said nothing to Tony Russo. I avoided Billy Kotlowitz. I stopped going to mass. Then one morning Tommy called me down into the "garden." He was in a state of evident panic. Billy had been arrested the night before, dressed in a bra and ladies' panties, on a fire escape outside someone's bedroom window.

My heart raced. Like Tommy, I panicked, without knowing what I was panicked about. For days afterwards I walked around overcome by shame— for having held Billy's body to mine (not because I suddenly thought he might be gay, something so secret I knew nothing of it—but rather because I thought of him now as soiled by sex and somehow contagious), for having held Billy's dirty pictures, for having held myself . . . for my criminal sinfulness.

I was forbidden the basement. Tommy and I stopped seeing each other. For days I slunk around as though I had been branded, as though everyone surely could tell at a glance that I had been marked "Guilty Alien" and could never belong. I never went to confession again.

A great many years later, when my own children were pushing into adolescence, it finally dawned on me that what had happened was yet another of those "Only in America" things. In some way hasn't every American fallen from grace, and don't we all want to deny it, evade it, repress it? Image and reality—what could be more obvious?--have never meshed, especially in this place that for almost all of us has had to be *made* into home, such disenchanting work. Bred on all those big ideas (salvation by election, Manifest Destiny . . .), we are hopelessly, endlessly starry-eyed and find the disenchantment almost impossible to live with. It's an indication of how hard I, anyway, found it to abandon the dream of a sanctified destiny that even all those years later, when I thought I had begun to get a handle on it all, even then it did not cross my mind that it might be ok just to live. Maybe because that's a genuinely unAmerican idea.

I was right, by the way, about Buster Brown. About a year or so after we settled in Inwood the store closed. First there was a closeout sale, then a pile of boxes and legless chairs appeared on the sidewalk in front of the store, as if a family delinquent on its rent had just been evicted. Sure enough there was the X-ray box, gutted of its innards and looking all the more like a miniature coffin. I wanted to grab it and take it home. But I knew I couldn't. There was nothing I could do to turn the broken thing I had loved back again into a magical contraption.

HORATIO HORNBLOWER[1]: ON READING

C. S. Forester published the first of the Horatio Hornblower books that I read, *Lieutenant Hornblower*, in 1952, the year that my family and I arrived in the United States (the first book of the saga Forester wrote, however—*Beat to Quarters*—came out in 1939). It is the first book I read in English, and it is the book that made me a reader. I came across it entirely by accident at the Inwood public library up on Broadway one block north of my junior high school, P.S. 52 Manhattan (Alberto Manguel, in his wonderful *A History of Reading*, says that "largely [his] encounters with books have been

---

1 The Hornblower Saga includes these eleven books, published in paperback in 1999 by Back Bay Books, an imprint of Little, Brown and Company: *Mr. Midshipman Hornblower; Lieutenant Hornblower; Hornblower and the* Hotspur; *Hornblower During the Crisis; Hornblower and the* Atropos; *Beat to Quarters; Ship of the Line; Flying Colours; Commodore Hornblower; Lord Hornblower;* and *Admiral Hornblower in the West Indies.*

a matter of chance".[2]) Perhaps it was on display as a new release. I liked to hang around the library after school because as the only child of working parents I found our empty apartment in the late afternoons cold and lonely. I don't have any recollection of the physical appearance of the book, but it must have been a new hardback, for I picked it up shortly after it was published. In contrast the Hornblower books I now own are in the handsome eleven-volume Back Bay Books paperback set. The jacket illustrations of these books pose one of the first questions that seem to come up immediately about the books that have made readers readers: Is this a book for children or adults?

There is a whole intriguing subset of books that were written originally for adults, and that sit pretty high on everyone's list of great books, that none-theless became—at any rate for a time—books for children. I am thinking of books like *Gulliver's Travels, Robinson Crusoe, Pride and Prejudice, Jane Eyre,* and some (or many) of Dickens' books or Jack London's. The Hornblower books, clearly, are not books of this sort. They are more like Wells' *The War of the Worlds* (a book Forester was extremely fond of, and that he had read before he was ten) or Robert Louis Steven-

2 Alberto Manguel, *A History of Reading* (New York: Penguin Books, 1997), 20.

son's *Kidnapped*. I own the Penguin Classic edition of *Kidnapped*, and its cover has the same ambiguous qualities as do the covers of my Hornblower books. Like *Kidnapped*, the Hornblower books are set in one of the most romantic historical periods, at least for the purposes of historical fiction—the final defeat of the Jacobite cause in 1746, in the former case, and the Napoleonic wars, in the latter. And so we find men in strange dress (and especially strange headgear) wielding swords on the covers of both books. The rendering on the cover of *Kidnapped* is in faded colors and foggy detail while the Hornblower illustrations are sharp and made to appear as etchings—but in both cases there's a swashbuckling tone to the whole thing that tells you these are books of action or adventure, popular books, books full of excitement, romance (in the broad sense of the term), and promise—that might be read by children and/or by adults. The books that have made readers readers seem to inhabit this borderland or twilight zone, and I want to consider a little what this might mean.

The author of the only scholarly study of Forester, Sandford Sternlicht, says that there were two main heroes of twentieth century "escapist fiction": Hornblower, and James Bond. "Forester and Fleming," Sternlicht argues, "captured the hidden self-images of their times," Forester for the World War II generation and Fleming for the Cold War generation.[3] Sternlicht seems to be saying that in the 40s and 50s the public persona of Western culture—by implication dull, upstanding, conformist—masked a much more adventurous communal inner self. But on a little probing Sternlicht's phrase "hidden self-images" becomes more puzzling. Can Sternlicht mean that most of us see ourselves secretly as Hornblower or Bond? I'd say that's extremely unlikely. But we may wish we were, or we may slip away from war or cold war into fantasies that we are.

In this sense—reading as escape—the archetypal young reader, to my mind, is Jane Eyre, hidden in her window seat behind the red moreen curtain, clasping her volume of Bewick, and traveling by force of dread or imagination to Nova Zembla (an island, it turns out, in Baffin Bay near Greenland) or exotic scenes of crime and mystery (later, though I find this hard to believe, she says she found the same thrills in *Pamela* and *Henry, Earl of Moreland*. In any event her reading was prophetic, for she *did* marry her master. Although Jane is maybe being a little

3 Sanford Sternlicht, *C.S. Forester* (Boston: Twayne Publishers, 1981), preface.

bold here. Charles Lamb tells the story of reading *Pamela* one day on Primrose Hill when a friend— "a familiar damsel"—finds him and sits by him, wanting to read along. "There was nothing in the book," he says, "to make a man seriously ashamed at the exposure; but as she seated herself down by me, and seemed determined to read in company, I could have wished it had been—any other book." Soon enough his friend is embarrassed and leaves. "Gentle casuist, I leave it to thee to conjecture, whether the blush (for there was one between us) was the property of the nymph or the swain in this dilemma."[4]. Jane is driven to her nook by her position as outcast: this however is the position of every reader, isn't it, and in particular of every young reader (Manguel writes that "readers are bullied in schoolyards and in locker rooms as much as in government offices and prisons" [21])? Jane is at once escaping from something she knows well and fears and despises, and escaping to a place in the mind that she doesn't really have adequate experience of but that all of her instincts tell her is the

---

4 The impulse to read *Pamela* in unexpected places, and outdoors, seems to have struck Virginia Woolf, too: "The only peaceful places in the whole city," she writes in an essay on "Abbeys and Cathedrals," "are perhaps those old graveyards which have become gardens and playgrounds. . . . Here one might sit and read *Pamela* from cover to cover." See Virginia Woolf, *The London Scene: Six Essays on London Life* (New York: HarperCollins, 1975), 50-51.

right place for her. Because this is about looking for home in all the wrong places, both movements have something of wickedness about them. The OED quotes Darwin's use of an all-but-lost meaning of "escape" as a blunder or peccadillo (especially in the sense of a "breach of chastity"): "Now you may quiz me," he is quoted as saying, "for so foolish an escape of mouth." Jane's hope to escape the cruelty of the Reed household is a blunder as is her delight in her imaginary travels, for she is soon found out; the very object of her escape is flung at her head by John Reed, and draws blood. Now, however, in unaccustomed rebellion, she lets fly, and flings back at the Reeds words that are truly foolish escapes of mouth. For the first time she tastes the narcotic high you get from wielding a sharp metaphorical knife. And its bitter aftertaste.

(Like Forester a century later, Charlotte Bronte—a more extreme case than her heroine of reading to escape—took liberties with Wellington's family, the Wellesleys, using the family name as a pen-name for an early novel, *The Green Dwarf* , and naming the hero of her childhood epic, *Tales of Angria,* Arthur Augustus Adrian Wellesley, Duke of Zamorna. She loved Scott above all novelists, and the Duke of Wellington above all men. We have this information from Bronte's biographer, Elizabeth Gaskell, who tells us about her own early reading that because she was raised in the countryside at Knutsford by old people who only had old books in the house, she read as a girl and loved Henry Brooke's *The Fool of Quality*, which as it happens John Wesley abridged into the book that thrilled Jane Eyre under the title *Henry, Earl of Moreland*.)

I should perhaps pause at this point and, to fill in the back story, say a few words about my own particular circumstances at the time I first picked up *Lieutenant Hornblower*. The most important thing to say is that I was born in Slovakia in 1941 to Jewish parents. More or less everything follows from that at once wholly accidental and yet fateful fact of origin. We lived in a small town around thirty miles north of the Slovak capital, Bratislava. It was an unremarkable backwoods town, with the Catholic Church on one side of the town square and the synagogue on the other. The only person of note in the town's history was the father of Franz Liszt, who was born there. Through luck, the goodwill and occasionally the reckless bravery of others, and my father's indefatigable resourcefulness, we (my mother, father, and I) survived the Holocaust—first living right on the town's main street (my father was a "Jew Necessary to the Economy"), and then, for about nine months, in a hamlet and bunkers in the Little Carpathian mountains.[5] More or less everyone else from the town who was Jewish, and who had not had the foresight or good fortune to have fled, perished. Among the dead were all but one of my father's seven siblings, his mother (his father had abandoned the family and emigrated years earlier), my mother's one sister, and her parents. Today there are no Jews in my hometown; the synagogue is a "cultural center."

After the War we lived for five years in Quito, Ecuador before finally arriving in the United States and settling in the very northern tip of Manhattan, in an apartment on west 205th street, a stone's throw from the Harlem River. I missed out on the common—and as far as I can tell universally loved—experience of having had stories read to me as a child, and I did not read any children's literature. Perhaps the long traveling among strangers and strange languages made choosing books for me impossible for my parents. In any event it did not happen, and I first read for pleasure—and, in the way these things seem to happen, was wholly

5 See my memoir under the pen name Jiri Wyatt: *Against Capitulation* (London: Quartet Books, 1984).

swallowed up by—C.S. Forester's Hornblower books.

The Gothic fascination that drew Jane Eyre to Bewick was not what drew me to Hornblower. Jane, trapped in her enclosure in the cold north of England, longing for escape, found comfort in Bewick's exotic locales, and the farther from her world, and the stranger the scene, the greater her thrill. I had seen more than enough of exotic locales; I had no desire to wander. On the contrary, I wanted to settle and bring my time as an outcast to an end. At the same time, I too, like Jane (and Charlotte Bronte), was looking for home—and I found it more or less as she did. Ferndean, the house Jane at last settles in with the blasted Rochester, and where she begins a family with him, is really a locale out of the Bewick Jane loved as a girl: the novel ends in a place very much like the place where it begins. Ferndean is best thought of as a reading nook, for it is not a house in anything you might call a neighborhood, a place with actual neighbors and dinners with company and that sort of reassuring, homely routine, but rather, more or less in every sense of the term, an escape, a place in the middle of the wood, the sort of place where Dante seeks Beatrice, a place in the mind.

And so, reading the Hornblower stories now, I
can immediately see both how they appealed to me,
and then how they offered me many things I didn't
know to ask for. And let me say how lucky I was
not to have picked up *Casino Royale* instead, the first
Bond novel, which appeared in 1953. Hornblower's
naval universe is a great place to run to—it is an
"escape" without being altogether a fantasy (whereas
the Bond novels are obviously, and wildly, fantastic).
Forester's method, which is to narrate as though he
were reporting mere historical happenings, gives the
Hornblower books, once you grant their premises
and volunteer a suspension of disbelief, a certain
substance, a form of reality, and for a boy part of
the unexpected qualities of this reality are the moral
ones. Here, for example, is the first paragraph of
Lieutenant Hornblower :

Lieutenant William Bush came on
board H. M. S. *Renown* as she lay at anchor
in the Hamoaze and reported himself to
the officer of the watch, who was a tall
and rather gangling individual with hollow
cheeks and a melancholy cast of counte-
nance, whose uniform looked as if it had

been put on in the dark and not readjusted since.

This gangling, melancholy individual is Hornblower. Now the boy I am trying to conjure up, the Slovak boy lately come to Manhattan from South America, with his failing knowledge of Slovak and small knowledge of Spanish and English, and with his nonexistent knowledge of the greater world, this boy was a neat dresser, the only tidy thing about him, because his mother was a seamstress, and very particular. He will have noticed, with a mixture of emotions, Hornblower's ramshackle appearance, just as he must have been baffled by most of the rest of the paragraph, beginning with "H. M. S." (yes, it's a ship, but what can the letters stand for?) and the odd-looking "Hamoaze" (which I bet, dear reader, you too know nothing about) but continuing to "gangling" and "melancholy" (which perhaps by now, if you're anyplace near my age, is an old friend?).

The narrative perspective at the opening—and then at the close—of *Lieutenant Hornblower* is unusual, for almost always Forester narrates his stories in the indirect first person, sitting on Hornblower's shoulder from a sort of omniscient distance. But here, luckily for the Slovak boy first reading the book, Forester lets us look at Hornblower through someone else's eyes, and for a time the reader sees him and everything else from Bush's reliable, stolid, but downright mundane point of view. (First-time readers would not know that in every book Bush is to Hornblower as Watson is to Holmes.) Fleming also narrates in the indirect first person. But there the similarities end. Forester's English is the great plain style of the public school boy of the early twentieth century, and is the same English you find in the writing of Bertrand Russell and Leonard Woolf and John Maynard Keynes and Graham Greene. It's an English grown up along exercises in Latin, of a certain structural rigor and rhythmic muscle, and in that sense athletic, no-nonsense, with an exact but never fancy vocabulary, and an air of inherited authority appropriate to inherited wealth (even when the writer has no wealth and is a Socialist, like Leonard Woolf). And although Fleming went to Eton, he writes a debased version of this English; and whereas everything in Forester is credible, and in fact the beauty of his narratives is that you receive them as reports of actual events by a redoubtable observer, little in Fleming is credible, and for the most part what he tells us is silly when not ridiculous, and is only salvaged in the Bond movies, with their witty self-mockery. Here is a little philosophy from James Bond as he's about to take on the notorious Le Chiffre at baccarat:

> Above all, he liked it that [in gambling] everything was one's own fault. There was only oneself to praise or blame. Luck was a servant and not a master. Luck had to be accepted with a shrug or taken advantage of up to the hilt. But it had to be understood and recognized for what it was and not confused with a faulty appreciation of the odds, for, at gambling, the deadly sin is to mistake bad play for bad luck. And luck in all its moods had to be loved and not feared. Bond saw luck as a woman, to be softly wooed or brutally ravaged, never pandered to or pursued. But he was honest enough to admit that he had never yet been made to suffer by cards or by women. One day, and he accepted the fact, he would be brought to his knees by love or by luck. When that happened he knew that he too would be branded with the deadly question mark he recognized so

often in others, the promise to pay before
you have lost:the acceptance of fallibility.[6]

Although this is tawdry, it does reveal one of the
main motives for reading, especially of those books
that have made readers readers, and this is the
desire for guidance. It may be curious, a paradox,
that you should go to escape fiction for guidance,
but nevertheless that's the way it is. The point is
perhaps more obvious in the case, say, of Jane Eyre,
or me at age twelve, for to learn what we needed
to we had only books to go to since there was no
example in the adult world to follow, in Jane's case
on account of the perverse morality of her various
guardians, and in mine because my parents had
even less purchase on the ins and outs of the New
World than I. In this sense it is as if every young
reader is Huck Finn, whose moral examples are his
father the town drunk, on the one hand, and his
hopelessly strait-laced guardians, on the other, and
who therefore has to find his way on his own. At its
most obvious, the guidance we want from books is
about what "H. M. S." stands for, or on which side
of the plate to put the forks, or how to address the
Lord of the Manor, and more of the same. (The

---

6 Ian Fleming, *Casino Royale* (New York: Penguin Books, 2002), 042 (sic).

42

Hamoaze, incidentally, is a stretch of estuary that runs past the Devonport Dockyard, which belongs to the Royal Navy.) More broadly, and deeply, the guidance one seeks in books is about how to get on in the world, how to manage one's initiation or rite of passage, a process that obviously applies to the young person coming of age, but that can as well, in a more profound sense, have to do with becoming an adult, which is perhaps a process without an age limit (and so the books that end with a marriage, and the books that begin with a marriage; or, books for children, and books for adults).

What makes *Jane Eyre* a book that can be read happily by children is that on the novel's first page its heroine is a child of ten, and her trials and triumphs from that point on are equally bracing. If the novel has been abbreviated or otherwise edited, the power of the plot becomes all the more exciting and trium- phant, but even unabridged the novel can electrify the young reader despite the fact that he or she may be unable to follow some of the book's conflicts, themes, or plot lines to their adult conclusions. Injustice, especially injustice wedded to hypocrisy, is a sure draw for the young reader (apparently we all feel hard done by as kids). Insofar as *Jane Eyre* can be a book for children, it is a book with a definite ending and unequivocal resolutions. The reason, however, that some things are not fit for children is not they are too violent or too raunchy but too ambivalent. The child who encounters the reality that things may or may not work out for the best too early is a child whose childhood has been blasted. The books *intended* for children build up to a definite ending, something like an enormous, dense wall. An adult finds in these books pretty much what a child does. Not only can these books not be open-ended, they do not open out onto any vista; they are not about becoming but about being, being twelve, let's say, or thirteen. It may be that even if we open these books to escape, once we begin reading we encounter ourselves in ways we had not expected to (as Jane does in Bewick). Nevertheless the adult who reads *Jane Eyre* will read even as triumphant a book as this one, as he or she will read every great book, that is, with a sinking heart. The inescapably tragic qualities of human *being*, its rudimentary incompleteness, its curious, exasperating embodiment, its slavery to drives and instincts and passions, not to mention, as Helen Burns insists on mentioning, our mortality—all this forbids not necessarily a happy ending, but finality. There is something of Coleridge's Wedding Guest in every adult reader, and once the tale is told we return to our everyday world wiser, yes, and vivified by art, but also sadder.

Forester thought of the Hornblower books as books for adults; to him they are psychological studies of, as he puts it, "man alone." I don't know whether he cribbed this from Conrad, but if he did he misunderstood Conrad, who was interested in failure, and who (like Becket after him) saw every human endeavor as a failure (*The Heart of Darkness* has not been abridged for kids), whereas Forester, who writes after all as an entertainer, is interested in success. In Forester's books success means a successful course of action, problem-solving in small and large ways, and leadership. He is in fact intensely interested in the details of action, an area of manliness that only enters Conrad's books on the level of philosophy: we know that Marlow believes he is distinguishable from Kurtz because he has things to do, a routine to keep, but in truth we never see him doing these things as we do Hornblower.

(Forester loves the accessories of the manly life, and his vocabulary is full of the relish of naming, a delight given extra spice by period detail. When Hornblower first appears on deck in the opening of *Beat to Quarters*, we learn that "Brown, the captain's coxswain, had seen to it that the weather side of the quarterdeck had been holystoned and sanded at the first peep of daylight." The deck is sanded because Hornblower takes his daily walk there. "On one hand his walk was limited by the slides of the quarterdeck carronades; on the other by the row of ringbolts in the deck for the attachment of the carronade train tackles . . ." And there's plenty more of the same in every book and on practically every page of the Hornblower saga.)

Hornblower's success though, attractive as it is to the young reader, is hardly a one-dimensional matter. He's not made of wood, and he's not a cliché. When Bush first meets him, in the opening pages of *Lieutenant Hornblower*, Hornblower is fiercely berating the acting gunner, Hobbs, and his manner, at least momentarily, gives Bush a wrong impression.

Bush was making a mental note that this Hornblower was a firebrand when he met his glance and saw to his surprise a ghost of a twinkle in their melancholy depths. In a flash of insight he realized that this fierce young lieutenant was not fierce at all, and that the intensity with which he spoke was entirely assumed—it

was almost as if Hornblower had been
exercising himself in a foreign language.(4)

Not too much later we find Hornblower is green with
seasickness; and in each of the books we learn too that
he is squeamish about, and thoroughly uncomfortable with, corporal punishment. Now Hornblower,
a great leader of men, is always in the company of
others, his inferiors and his superiors, friends and
enemies, women and men. Forester provides us, that
is, with ample evidence of how others respond to
exactly the same dilemmas, dangers, opportunities,
triumphs, and defeats as Hornblower does. Bush's
insight reveals that Hornblower's leadership is
thoroughly self-conscious: what makes him a great
leader, morally, is that he assumes as a matter of
course that he must lead (rather than that he can
lead; Hornblower's pervasive sense of responsibility would be much diminished if it all came to
him naturally) and that he acts therefore as each
situation demands. He can be self-effacing, or fierce,
or obsequious all depending on what is necessary to
get the job done. As it happens, Hornblower's many
other gifts, including a formidable diligence, always
beyond the call of duty, and a supple intelligence,
make him a man others trust and lean on; but for

the reader, especially the young reader, it's his moral qualities that are most engaging, and instructive.

Still, there's something upsetting about the thought that Hornblower, in telling Hobbs off, was practicing a foreign language. A reader who had followed the stories from *Beat to Quarters* on would have been thoroughly familiar with Hornblower by the time he came to *Lieutenant Hornblower*, and would have known more or less everything there was to know about the man's character, abilities, and habits. Perhaps displaying Hornblower's leadership had grown tiresome to Forester (*Lieutenant Hornblower* is the seventh novel in the saga). In any event, it's clear that to Forester a leader is a man who must always play his part, and who to succeed must know how to use his part to achieve victory. But the suggestion that the language of leadership is foreign to Hornblower clashes with what we know of him; in fact, although he is not a man of steel, or whatever would be the appropriate stereotype, he has an unusual gift for this language, and takes to it readily. That, after all, is what differentiates him from the other, frequently quite capable, characters in the novels, and from us.

At the same time thinking of being a man as a language that can be learned is enormously reassuring as well as seductive, especially to the young reader (who I assume is likely to be male). The form of courage most often displayed in the novels is overcoming one's fears. In particular, Hornblower—unassuming, generous, tender-hearted—shows that the man alone—Forester's pedagogic model for how to be a man—is someone who does what he must, whether he likes it or not, and (of course) without complaint; if he must climb up a mast even though it makes him dizzy, he will do so without hesitation, just as he will exact punishment even though it makes him wince (inwardly), obey orders with grace even though he thinks them wrong, and drink fetid ship's water with relish, because to do otherwise would demoralize the men . . . When I started reading Hornblower I was still waking most nights screaming from recurring nightmares caused by my memories of the terrorizing sound of weapons being fired. I was told by my mother—for I don't remember this—that when we were still living openly in our home town in Slovakia, and she had taken me out in a carriage for a walk one day, planes appeared overhead. She says I said to her (I was three), "Don't let them kill me!" Some months later, when I was playing outside the second bunker in which we were hiding, now fairly deep in the Little Carpathians, a German soldier wandering through the woods spotted me and fired his rifle at me. Toward the end of our time in hiding, when we were living high in the mountains, in the fifth and most roomy of our hiding places, the final Russian assault passed directly over our cabin, an enormously loud barrage directed at the retreating German troops. My father refused to stay in the mountains until the Russian advance passed, and we left our hideout with me being pulled in a handcart in the midst of the half-wild Russian front-line soldiers, a bumpy, chaotic, and most of all fearfully noisy journey back to our hometown. These terrifying sounds of war have remained with me all my life, but only rarely after the age of fourteen or so did they blast me out of sleep. In the end I simply outgrew them, or perhaps I felt, finally, safe enough, and magically could no longer hear them. But in the meanwhile, I imagine it must have been very soothing to that uncertain Slovak boy to keep company with the upstanding Lieutenant Hornblower and *his* war-time terrors, and to believe too that not only were there things that even Horatio Hornblower was afraid of, but that these sorts of terrors, apparently common to us all, could be overcome.

In *Lieutenant Hornblower,* Hornblower and Bush are junior officers on board H.M.S. *Renown,* whose commanding officer, Captain Sawyer, is paranoid (actually paranoid), cruel, and, as the book establishes almost at once, unfit for command. I said earlier that injustice is a sure draw for the young reader, and Pip, in Dickens' *Great Expectations,* explains exactly why this is so. The way his sister raised him, he says, made him "sensitive. In the little world in which children have their existence whosoever brings them up, there is nothing so finely perceived and so finely felt, as injustice. It may be only a small injustice . . . but the child is small, and its world is small." In Pip's case injustice took the form of the "capricious and violent coercion" he suffered at the hands of his sister, that he suffered, as he puts it, "in a solitary and unprotected way," with the result that he "was morally timid and very sensitive."[7]

I too was morally timid and very sensitive. In my case the injustice—though I would not have used the word, or recognized it as applicable—was

---

7 Penguin Classics, 1996; 63.

also capricious and violent. Capricious, violent, but impersonal, and for that reason liable to the most satisfying trouncing not in life but in art. In *Lieutenant Hornblower* Captain Sawyer's incapacity for command so exasperates his officers that they arrange a clandestine meeting to talk things over, the only time Hornblower is ever seen to be willing to plot against authority. But as it happens, on his way to uncover the plot in the dark lower decks, the Captain stumbles down a hatchway and dies of his injuries. Hornblower is the first to find him, and we are lead to believe—or, in any event, we are not discouraged from thinking—that Hornblower might well have pushed the Captain to his death.

Something I could never have done, and in the reading, as an adult, still find it hard fully to imagine. In *Lieutenant Hornblower* Captain Sawyer's death doesn't raise any moral issues or doubts. The only question is whether there will be a suspicion of mutiny when the incident is investigated, and in that case what such an outcome might augur for Hornblower and his fellow officers. But the idea that injustice can be overcome by murder seems in the book—and of course, the *Renown* is a ship at war— to be a perfectly plausible course of action. Sawyer dies quite early in the book, and his death is followed by a series of adventures, as well as an uncharacteristic denouement (about which, more in a moment). Hornblower has no second thoughts, and we never learn what actually happened. Still, I don't think I could have done it, not then, when I first read the book; and I doubt I could do it now. I don't mean to suggest that the act was morally wrong, and I am repulsed by it; no, for there does not seem to be a standard to apply, let alone an absolute standard. Rather, the killing of the captain—if he *was* killed—brings you directly up against what might be called the Israeli dilemma. As the victim of caprice and violence, are you justified in using caprice and violence to prevent further caprice and violence?

In one of Tom Stoppard's brilliant short plays for TV, *Professional Foul* (1977), an Oxbridge professor travels to Prague, ostensibly to attend a linguistics conference but actually to catch a soccer game in the European Cup (one source for the title). A former student, Hollar, searches him out and asks him to smuggle his thesis on ethics to the West. The professor, a worldly and clever Oxbridge type, is uncertain, and in conversation with Hollar debates the rights and wrongs of doing what his student asks. Hollar tells him that when he is unsure of what's right and wrong he has a simple way of settling the matter: he asks his eight-year-old son. And indeed his thesis is based on the idea of "a sense of right and wrong that precedes utterance," a sense of "natural justice."

As a child, you believe—I believed—in this sense of natural justice. In childhood, when, as Dickens so poignantly puts it, the child is small and his world is small, injustice takes the form of, say, being cheated, or, as so often in Pip's life, of being accused of crimes you have not only not committed but could not have committed (such as having willed your birth to plague the adults). One's sense of being wronged is visceral and immediate—and we know it to be justified. But Magwitch, Miss Haversham, and Estella confuse things. In his encounters with these compelling but morally ambiguous persons, Pip feels . . . guilty. He is not so much guilty about anything in particular as he is afflicted with a Kafka-esque sense of guilt, one that is existential and, in the end, beyond any apparent cause. By doing the wrong thing for the right reasons—as when he steals food for Magwitch—Pip encounters a new kind of injustice. He is not being cheated, nor is he being falsely accused. In fact he accuses himself, or rather feels the emotion of self-accusation—guilt—at the same time that he loses his sense of natural justice, loses, that is, his bearings. The injustice is no longer something external, happening *to* him. Instead, the injustice seems to arise directly out of the circumstance of being Pip, that is, of being human. Pip's sadness, as an adult, is the residue of his guilt, and comes from his knowing that there is no natural justice, and worse, that once you have set off for Vanity Fair, as we all do and as we all must, there is no sure way to find your bearings.

A child of the Holocaust, if I am at all a fair example, is a child who knows two powerful truths: that without a sense of natural justice the world is mean, and life a soiled thing; and that survival requires capricious and violent coercion. As a boy, though, I was wholly incapable of capricious and violent coercion. I hated the idea that being a man meant throwing around your fists, and I resisted all assertions that the world is a shithole and I'd better start looking out for Number One, now! But my incapacity troubled me. It is obvious to every boy that the field of meaning is the playing field, which strictly obeys the rules of Darwinian natural selection and whose only morality is: survival of the fittest. It was salving to escape this tangle by living vicariously through Horatio Hornblower, who was steady, wily, tough-minded, but nonetheless good.

At least while he was out on the seas. On land however—and we find Hornblower on land infrequently—he is awkward, diminished, vulnerable, although still recognizably Hornblower. On land, his decisions are not always reliable, and he is, I guess I should say "of course," especially bad at relationships with women. In the closing sections of *Lieutenant Hornblower*, after a lot of daring and ingenious triumphs that earn Hornblower promotion to commander, we find him in poverty in a wintry Portsmouth. Peace with Napoleon has been signed, the great Royal Navy has been beached, its ships returned to port or worse, and its officers put on half pay. We now discover that Hornblower's promotion was never confirmed because peace broke out first, and he has therefore had to live without any regular income at all while he pays back the difference between his lieutenant's wages and the captain's pay he earned during his few months in command. Only then, still five months into the future at the time we meet him at Portsmouth, will he finally receive even half-pay. In the meantime he lives without an overcoat or much to eat, lodges in a cheap boarding house where he is behind on the rent, and keeps body and soul together through his earnings from games of whist at the Long Rooms, a military club in the port.

What might make others bitter, and might without exaggeration be taken as injustice, is accepted by Hornblower with stoicism, grace, and ingenuity. His ordeal is made a bit easier by the practical help and emotional solace he receives from Maria, the faintly dowdy daughter of his gorgon of a landlady. She mends and brightens his threadbare clothes, feeds him, and even slips money into his pockets, all of which is just about beyond bearing for the proud Hornblower. At the very end of the novel, when war is once more declared, and Hornblower is called again to command, poor Maria is crushed. She can't hold back, sobs that she wishes she were dead, and—this is the word Forester uses— wails in grief. Bush, who is witness to all this, voices our reaction: " 'Oh, for God's sake,'" he says, "in disgust." But Hornblower is incapable of being disgusted by another's grief, especially as he sees himself to be the cause of it, and especially if the grief is a woman's . . . and so, naturally, he marries her.

We know he marries her because of the coy pleasure Forester very clearly derives from this, the book's final paragraph:

> She gazed up at Hornblower with adoration shining in her face, and he looked down at her with infinite kindness. And already there was something a little proprietorial about the adoration, and perhaps there was something wistful about the kindness.

Which is not how Hornblower feels about Lady Barbara Wellesley, Wellington's sister. In *Beat to Quarters*, where Hornblower battles the Spanish off the coast of Central America, he is ordered to carry her, and her maid, home to England from Panama on his thirty-six gun warship, the *Lydia*. Hornblower has little occasion, as a seaman, to encounter women, but when he does it is almost always on shore. He meets Lady Barbara, uniquely, on board his ship. At first he is irritated to have to care for her; she is a distraction and he is at war. Before returning to England he has to take on the much bigger *Natividad*, which has fifty guns. In *Beat to Quarters*, the barbarity of battles at sea, in wooden boats that can barely protect the men, without adequate medicines or medical knowledge or even for that matter adequate ventilation—all this, with its brutality, bodily anguish, and loss of life, is baldly displayed. Hornblower expects the aristocratic Lady Barbara to be squeamish and spoiled, but she is neither, proves to be a compassionate but steely and martial companion, as well as an especially able nurse of the many ghoulishly wounded. They fall in love. But as the prospect of arrival at Portsmouth sinks in as an imminent reality, Hornblower finds that

> . . . the image of Maria had been much before his eyes of late; Maria, short and tubby, with a tendency to spots in her complexion, with the black silk parasol which she affected . . .

He thinks prudently, moreover, that the "Wellesley family could blast him at their whim . . . . To meddle with Lady Barbara would mean risking utter ruin." But "then all these cold blooded considerations were swept away to nothing again in a white hot wave of passion as he thought of her, slim and lovely . . . He was trembling with passion, the hot blood running under his skin . . ." Finally: "it was coincidence that his hand should brush against her bare arm as they stood cramped between the table and the locker . . . She was in his arms then, and they kissed, and kissed again." She tells him his hands are beautiful and that she has loved them ever since she boarded the ship. Hornblower, however, is for once paralyzed. " 'What are we to do?' he [asks] feebly [!]." He tells her: "I am a married man," and she replies, "I know that. Are you going to allow that to interfere with—us?" Hornblower hesitates. "She saw the look in his face, and rose abruptly. Her blood and lineage were outraged at this. However veiled her offer had been, it had been refused. She was in a cold rage now."

The setting is 1808; the publication date is 1939—dates that I bring up because the Hornblower books were enormously popular and so I think it's safe to say that Forester's treatment of relations between the sexes, and of sex, reflects the outlook of the time. There is something of the suggestion, here and there in the books when women appear, that the time in question is the Napoleonic era, and that, say, the sexual forthrightness of Lady Barbara can be attributed to her "lineage" as an aristocrat in an aris-tocratic age. One of my first surprises, on rereading the books, was to find not only that Hornblower had a wife but that his emotional and sexual passions are so directly and explicitly on show. From the point of view of guidance, though, the picture here is nothing like as clear as with Hornblower the leader of men. At sea Hornblower is always in command; but even at sea, his relation with Lady Barbara turns the tables of power. He is nonplussed; he is unsure of himself; he speaks *feebly*—all of these unthinkable under any other circumstance. It is as if the boy's fantasy of adventure can be persuasively turned adult in the theater of war, where human relations are molded by the fierce rules of necessity that every organization devoted to war rigidly imposes on all its members. The military code tells you exactly how to behave; but it seems entirely unclear how you're supposed to behave when a woman presses her leg against yours under the table. Hornblower mainly blushes and obliges. For the young reader all of this must be pretty confusing, and if the reader is a boy must confirm the troublesome credo that feelings should be kept at a distance, or better, hidden or suppressed, and that whatever happens with women is unfathomable and anyway an exception to the lucid, rule-bound, repressed and repressive world of men. Be a wiseguy but don't be a sissy.

On the other hand, or alongside this worldly moral, the Hornblower books—like all novels— appeal to an unworldly judgment, the judgment of a figure you might call the eternal reader. Hornblower's example is different for us as readers than it is for the characters in the novels because we know what's behind the façade. When he overcomes fears, or aversions, we know while those other fictional beings living with him don't know. This is the point not only of omniscience but of all narrative: we know the characters of fiction as we can never know another human being, and as others can never know us. Virtue, in fiction, is sanctioned, then, not along the lines of the usual rules of human relations, which depend upon society. Nor is virtue in fiction sanctioned by religion, by the Christian, Jewish, Islamic, Hindu . . . God, except by analogy or metaphoric reference. No, instead judgment—implicit but palpable and definitive—is rendered by the collective reader, a divinity present only in the act of reading but in whom the living and the dead, the readers who inhabit the very pages of the books they are reading, equally thrive. This collective conscience frowns upon, or in any event scrupulously examines, the ethos of the playing field: Charlotte Bronte was voicing its credo when she defended

Jane Eyre against the religious literary journals of her own time by saying: "Conventionality is not morality." This collective conscience, the eternal reader, favors the sensitive and morally rigorous over the unreflective doers, insists that truth is beauty and beauty truth (without bothering to declare just what this might mean), and holds the human heart to be most beautiful of all. The eternal reader does not insist on marrying for love but rather on being true to one's self, which is one version of its faith and is what D. H. Lawrence was talking about when he said, famously, that you have to be so religious to be a novelist.

After a time Maria dies and Hornblower marries Lady Barbara. *Commodore Hornblower* opens with Hornblower—now Captain Sir Horatio Hornblower—in his bath being made ready to receive the ceremonial welcome of the villagers of his new estate, Smallbridge. "Park and orchard and church were all his; he was the squire, a landed gentleman, owner of many acres, being welcomed by his tenantry . . . This was the climax of a man's ambition. Fame, wealth, security, love, a child [Richard, his one surviving child by Maria]—he had all that heart could desire. Hornblower, standing at the head of the steps as the parson droned on, was puzzled to find that he was still not happy. . . . he was contemplating the future with faint dismay; dismay at the thought of living on here, and positive distaste at the thought of spending the fashionable season in London . . ."

Just at the end of the ceremony a letter arrives from the Admiralty: he is to be made Commodore and to report immediately for instructions. He is giddy with excitement: "this life here in Smallbridge or in Bond Street need not continue." He orders his best uniform and sword, the horses and the chariot . . . before he notices that Barbara has all the while been standing next to him. "God, he had forgotten all about her in his excitement, and she was aware of it." But she puts a brave face on it (of course), and tells him, "And you will come back to me." "Of course I will," he responds.

Okay, so this sort of thing goes back to Penelope and Odysseus. Domesticity is the harbor from which the hero sails out into the great world, and to which he returns. Adventure and domesticity are inextricable, and although this is obvious in the books of adventure, it's essential too to the main tradition of the novel in English, which reverses the center and the periphery, or better the canvas and the frame, making domesticity primary and adventure something out there. At the same time adventure can be incorporated into the domestic, though this can be dangerous and unsettling (as in *Wuthering Heights* or *The Sound and the Fury*). In the Hornblower books, though, not to get distracted, Forester lets us down softly from our visions of escape. Life in Smallbridge and Bond Street may seem miserable to Hornblower, who loves nothing better than to be risking his neck out at sea, but even the Slovak boy who read Forester's novels with utter unreflective absorption knew that life at sea was not for him. He didn't want to kill anybody, and knew he'd have to settle . . . well, but to settle where? to settle how?

II.

Writing (mostly) About Friends

SOME WORDS FOR/ON PHILIP ROTH

Prologue (Alas)

A t the date of this writing (July 2021) I am wondering whether Philip—whom I first met in the summer of 1978—is laughing or crying. He didn't want his posthumous reputation to be consumed by quarrels about just how Jewish he was, or wasn't, never mind by quarrels about whether he was or wasn't a serial abuser of women. He wanted to be remembered, and judged, as an *American* writer, period. Well, the fickle gods obviously had other plans. Philip's deliberate choice of a biographer has brilliantly backfired, muddying what Philip obviously anticipated would be a messy process of reassessment, one he hoped, or even expected (hope against hope), to shape and maybe control through Blake Bailey's biography.

Guess not.

Now, following the scandal about Bailey's harassment of women, you can no longer venture to say anything about Philip Roth's writing without also saying something about the relation of his life to his art.

So, since it's inescapable, here goes:

I first read the story "Good-bye, Columbus" not too long after it first came out, and at the time I didn't know anything about the writer, just as when today I read a story in, say, *The New Yorker* I usually don't know a thing about the writer. But I loved "Good-bye, Columbus" immediately, was stunned by the apparently effortless, classically plain narrative style, by the dialogue which, easily surpassing everything I'd read up to that point, so completely captured the way I heard people actually talk, and of course by the trenchantly upending plot. And I did not think then, and do not think now, that knowing details of the writer's life as a walking, talking, tax paying individual would do very much, never mind something fundamental, to enhance my experience of the story.

My view, then, is that for the most part the work should be read for itself, should stand on its own as a piece of writing. If the work is misogynistic, that invites and requires scrutiny. But the evidence seems to me pretty clear that whether people are, in life, good or bad or heroic or barbarous is unlikely (though, yes, there are exceptions) to help us appreciate or understand their work. (We don't know anything about Homer, if there was a Homer, and very little about Shakespeare or the writers of *Genesis*. So?)

But, as I've already said, since there's no escape from having to say something about Philip the person in relation to Philip the writer, it's a lucky coincidence that what should be said has already been well said by Daphne Merkin (online in *n+1*, June 2021). I am going to pick out just two points from her essay for emphasis. First, that while Philip clearly had slept with many women he did not stalk, assault, or in any other way behave like a sexual predator. He was a "celebrity author" from his twenties, which is not at all a simple, not to say a productive thing for a writer to live with; but doubtless a consequence was that all his adult life women as much as men were attracted to him because of his celebrity. Nevertheless, with women just as with men, certainly from what I was able to observe, he was gracious, attentive, empathetic, loyal, and a lot of fun to be with. I don't know whether it could be said of Philip as it was said of Lord Byron—that no woman ever complained about having been to bed with him—but we can say that Philip's sexual encounters were consensual.

Merkin ends her essay with the main point, which is that what Philip cared about first and last was the writing. He was astonishingly disciplined, could write eight hours a day seven days a week, labored and labored over each of his sentences . . . Philip lived for his art.

* *

I have included here three pieces on Philip and his work. The first, an account of the Memorial for Philip held at the New York Public Library not long after his death, was not originally written for publication. The second is a review that appeared in *Partisan Review,* and the last a talk given as part of a panel at YIVO.

A memorial service in honor of Philip Roth
September 25, 2018

The setting was the Celeste Bartos Forum, which is a grand, glass-saucer-domed space in the New York Public Library, directly in front of you if you enter the building through the side door on 42nd Street. I had no idea the space existed—and, like everything else in that magnificent building—the hallways, the ceilings, the toilets—it is stunning, a vaulting, airy space seating maybe 500. But it was a rainy late afternoon, and the light that seemed to swoon down from the glass ceiling was faint and grey so you felt you were maybe in a dour, foggy boxing arena after the fight was over . . .

Who was there? In the row in front of me— Vartan Gregorian and Salman Rushdie (in the company of a beautiful and much younger African American woman who, judging by the greetings all round, must either be his wife or his regular companion); many people, dressed neatly but avoiding anything to suggest death, from the literary business (editors, agents, and of course writers); "ordinary" people with whom Philip had been close (I recognized a bookseller to whom Philip always gave multiple copies of signed first editions of his work, in order to keep the man's book business going; some of the young men and women whom Philip had hired over the years to cook for him; I sat next to a woman who was the daughter of Philip's childhood neighbors in Newark: apparently Philip had occasionally been her babysitter . . . but according to her—and this is very disappointing--there are no home movies of Philip as a babysitter. And on the other side of me was Jonathan Brent, a scholarly man who runs YIVO, and who, it turns out, was one of the people to whom Philip sent his manuscripts for response and critique before he packed them off to his publisher (a select group of which I was never a member . . .).

We were not exactly a room full of twenty-somethings. No, soon we would be going to the next memorial service, likely to be in honor of one of us in the room. And it looked to me as if everyone present enjoyed three good meals a day, owned plenty of sturdy shoes (it was, as I've said, raining), and probably swam or played tennis or could have or should have . . . Rather than a lot of horny bachelors, many (evidently long-married) couples.

Baldwin, in "Notes of a Native Son," says about the funeral service for his father that those in attendance met there a man they had not known and never encountered instead of the dead man they *had* known—but that they had hardly expected to meet *him*—this was an occasion for eulogies, it was not the man who was remembered but his mortal wrestling. At Philip's memorial, however, we *did* meet the man we had known, which was striking and, also, powerful and very moving.

At the same time, the entire event, so precisely reflecting our profound bafflement about death, tended toward a kind of congenial remembrance. Few of the speakers hazarded expressions of grief.

Joel Conarroe opened and closed the ceremonies (an old friend of Philip's from when they were both working at Penn, president for a long time, now emeritus, of the Guggenheim Foundation). He reported—but since this was a room of Philip's friends, everyone will have deduced this anyway—that Philip had carefully and methodically planned the memorial, and over the years had given Conarroe a new set of names, those who were in and those who were out, and slightly altered orders of speakers, and of musical codas (what we got, at the end, was a few minutes of Gabriel Faure's beautiful *Elegie in C Minor, opus 24*).

It was not quite said by Conarroe, or by anyone, that Philip was a brilliant, not to say obsessive impresario of his career and reputation, and of his private and public persona. One example: In one of my conversations with Philip on the phone when he was staying at his (summer) house in northern Connecticut—I don't remember the year—he told me he had recently got himself some kittens. "Really," I said, not a little incredulous. He reported that they were very cute, but he had had to get rid of them. "Oh? Why?" He said he had enough to do to take care of himself: he didn't want to take care of anyone else, including a couple of very cute kittens. Variants of this story were told by a number of the speakers at the memorial. Philip during those years had retreated to Connecticut to write, and the story in the version of some speakers became a story about his singular devotion to his work, his discipline, his self-imposed isolation necessary to the struggle to produce, say, *American Pastoral.*

Now, Philip clearly told the story of the kittens to a great many people. It was something he had chosen to tell us as news of his life at that time, and he had it formulated and ready for use in conversation after conversation. In the same way, he did not give interviews unless he could edit what he'd said before the interviewer submitted the piece for publication.

And yet none of us seemed in the least miffed about the fact that, in what we thought of as casual and intimate conversation, Philip was actually promoting a certain calculated narrative about himself, a narrative he was promoting with everyone else who happened to have his phone number. The thing is his meticulous care for his "image" miraculously escaped seeming manipulative or exploitative but instead looked to be a kind of thoroughness none of the rest of us—and in fact no one else—ever lived up to. He had no one to do it for him: he had to do it himself. (And so we thought of this side of Philip with affection!) He could be just as meticulous, by the way, in caring for the reputations, the books, the jobs, the living arrangements of his friends (he was extremely loyal. You couldn't get him to praise or promote what he didn't think was up to scratch: but once committed, he was absolutely committed.).

After Conarroe Claudia Roth Pierpont spoke and then Norman Manea. Pierpont, who sometimes writes for *The New Yorker* and whom Philip clearly was very fond of, had written, under Philip's strict supervision, a truly terrible book about Philip, *Roth*

Unbound, that Philip touted passionately. Norman is another matter, something like a towering figure and yet at the same time completely endearing. He is looking frail—walks unsteadily, uses a cane—I kidded him about the cane—he said it was essential—"You see, my wife beats me"—He and Philip met soon after Norman managed to slip free of the grip of the Romanian secret police—he was allowed, as the greatest living Romanian writer, to emigrate—and landed in New York City. He told the story of their first meeting at Essex House, where Philip and Claire Bloom were staying (I assume they were waiting for their apartment across from the Natural History Museum to get ready for them). Norman had written something about Proust. Philip greeted him by pooh-pooing Proust—"Celine is my Proust." In Romania, Norman said, Proust *was* literature; and Celine was a well-known anti-Semite. He said to his wife Cella upon leaving that they would never see Philip again. But in fact Philip was very concerned about Norman—he took care to follow up on how Norman was doing, made sure he met people—he invited Marianne and me to a dinner to meet Norman and Cella at that time at some Italian restaurant in midtown (Philip frequented a particular class of restaurant all the years I knew him: nondescript places without pretensions where the food was OK but nothing to brag about, places where no celebrities would be caught dead, but places that would greet him with, "Good evening, Mr. Roth.")

But as it happened Norman and Philip grew very close over time, just as Norman had become very close to Saul Bellow. When visiting Philip in hospital this last time, Norman said, Philip told him he'd like to be buried near him in the cemetery at Bard so that he could have some entertaining company in the afterlife. They had competed for years, Norman said, about who had the most stints in the valves of his heart. Philip was in the lead with thirteen; he had always, true to character, triumphed over his infirmities. Except this time.

Another through-line in people's speeches: Philip's wit, playfulness, and humor (Jewish, of course). Bernie Avishai, Philip's agent Andrew Wylie, and Ben Taylor especially told or retold jokes. Wylie, head shaved, dramatic, told the story of Philip's marriage: Claire wanted to get married, Philip didn't. Finally Philip told her, I'll marry you when Nelson Mandela gets out of jail. So, Wylie says, I am watching the images on TV of Mandela leaving prison. The phone rings. It's Philip: "I'm fucked! I'm fucked! I'm fucked!" The marriage, Wylie says, didn't last. Wylie also told the story of the kittens (as did Judith Thurman). Taylor told the story of Mrs. Finkelstein. Mrs. Finkelstein has made it all the way through to the ultimate question of "The $64,000 Question." "So, Mrs. Finkelstein, for $64,000—Who was the first man?" (The following needs a Yiddish accent:) "Not for a *million* dollars would I tell you."

Nicole Kraus was due to speak but had to cancel at the last minute. Janis Freedman Bellow, Bellow's widow, spoke. I had last seen her I don't know where when she was not long married to Saul and had just had a child—maybe through Edith Kurzweil and the *Partisan Review* —she is a woman with a jaunty manner and a long stride, what Ford Madox Ford liked to call "clean run"—she spoke of receiving Philip's manuscripts for comment, addressed both to Saul and to her; how Philip would attend to what she thought, take notes, sometimes object. After Saul died the manuscripts continued to come, addressed now only to her: and the same, meticulous attention.

Judith Thurman spoke about Philip's intense focus, a quality many of those at the podium touched on—how he would become totally absorbed in what you were saying, stare at you unblinking, unsmiling, as though he was not just absorbing every scintilla of what you were saying, but appraising it in each of its parts. You felt—I felt—I had better have something genuine to say; in particular, no bullshit.

Then a person I didn't know or know of—Julia Golier, "co-literary executor of the estate of Philip Roth," also identified as an "Associate Professor of Psychiatry at Mount Sinai." Neither beautiful nor not beautiful, neither eloquent nor not eloquent, at moments overcome with emotion, she spoke with her eyes fixed on her text in the monotone that students often use to read out loud, as though to veil from us the woman Philip saw. For, it turned out, they had been together for a good while. They did the usual things, they traveled to Connecticut; in the evenings they played gin rummy. Then she moved on, met her husband, had two children—and Philip came over and played, engrossed, with the kids— maybe—at last?—glimpsing the domestic life he was never able to have.

And after Julia Golier, Edna Obrien, three years Philip's senior, a friend from his time in London in the seventies, when I too saw Philip in London. Back then Edna was not only a great writer but also a great beauty, a match for Philip in every way. There were rumors back then and down over the years that they had been lovers—at Philip's 80th birthday party in Newark O'Brien declared emphatically it was not so. They were, however, for my money, the two best stylists in the English-speaking world: now there is only Edna O'Brien.

Edna O'Brien—and Norman--stood out from the crowd in a way that I don't want to exaggerate but . . . There was something of the air, among this crowd, of being the best and the brightest, good people of good intentions at the top of their games—but just that little bit smug and self-satisfied, untested by the kind of brute conditions of life that O'Brien grew up with in the Ireland of her youth, and that Norman faced in wartime and postwar Romania.

I have been surprised, in the month since his death, by how much I miss Philip--on a personal level—we saw each other every few months for 40 years—but also because—as a follow-up to my remark above—Philip was the center of a wide network of people each of whom looked to him as the touchstone, the person who stood for American Literature. This network included a good cross section of the nation's most important editors, "opinion makers," and so forth. Philip's humor, judgment, outlook, standards, tact reverberated through this network of people, let's call it Philip's set. Now we are each of us left to our own devices, and the coherence of cultural life has been disturbed and dispersed just at the moment when the country could use a lot more coherence, judgment, and probity.

THE HUMAN STAIN. By Philip Roth.
Houghton Mifflin Company. 2000.

Philip Roth's latest novel, *The Human Stain*, forms the third, and perhaps concluding, volume of his recent, "historical" novels or chronicles (*American Pastoral* [1997] and *I Married a Communist* [1998]), while at the same time harking back to his great novella *The Ghost Writer*, published twenty years ago. All of these books are narrated by Nathan Zuckerman. In *The Ghost Writer* Zuckerman is a wide-eyed twenty-three-year-old writer, flush with his first success, on something of a pilgrimage to the New England backwoods (actually, the Berkshires) where in ascetic isolation his aesthetic father E.I. Lonoff has settled.

Now, in *The Human Stain*, Zuckerman has out-Lonoffed Lonoff. He has learned altogether too much about the writer's life and is happily launched into self-imposed exile in, yes, the Berkshires, aging, incontinent, impotent, living in a two-room cabin sans prostate, women, gerbils, dogs or cats, arrived at last at a spareness that Lonoff himself could have envied.

As a kind of monk Zuckerman is hardly at all an actor in the drama of the novel but rather a rapt listener to the stories of others, in particular to the story of his neighbor Coleman Silk, the long-time reforming dean of nearby Athena College. Silk, someone with whom Zuckerman has previously had no more than a nodding acquaintance, one day shows up on Zuckerman's doorstep and insists that he write the story of his (Silk's) career, which the dean himself has been trying to write without success, under the title *Spooks*. It turns out that, besides Lonoff, Silk has been the only other Jew on the Athena faculty and the only Jewish dean of faculty in the college's history. His reforming days abruptly ended by the departure of the college's president for a bigger job at a more imposing school, Silk returns to faculty after sixteen years out of the classroom as something of an anachronism (that is, as a Humanist) and soon enough his return explodes into scandal when he asks out loud about two students who have never showed up for his classics class—"Do they exist or are they spooks?" The two absent students, it appears, are black; Silk is accused of racism; foe and friend on the faculty wash their hands of him; in the fierce craziness that

ensues Silk's wife dies—*They* killed her! Silk rages . . .
You get the picture.

But in one of a number of wicked twists in the
novel, Zuckerman discovers that Silk has a secret
that puts everything in his story in an altogether
different light, in fact that Silk has more than one
secret. In fact each of the novel's characters harbors
a secret, some more or less banal, but some of the
kind that go to the very heart of identity.

A digression: The jacket of my copy of Roth's
second book, *Letting Go*, carries on the back a
picture of him that, when I first saw it (in 1962!),
produced in me a happy but also envious wave of
emotion. A meticulously trim and neat—and ridiculously young—Roth is sitting in a rocker facing the
camera. He has on a short-sleeve shirt open at the
neck, chinos, and what used to be called, before the
age of Nike, tennis shoes. On a low sidetable beside
him is what seems to be a board game, the name of
which you can make out to be Gettysburg.

So what's to be so emotional about? That
the guy—this Jewish boy from Jersey—could be so
palpably, photogenically American, so at ease in that
New England-y rocker, so relaxed about claiming the
culture (Gettysburg) for himself, so on top of goyishe

informality, and yet—as the sneakers seemed to say in particular—so much, so simply, so autonomously, so *already* himself! That the guy seemed—to me, an immigrant survivor of the Holocaust with a new Americanised family name—to have beautifully, easefully overcome all the thorns and messes of having to pass. The autonomy was a heady thing, to smile about; the sense of feeling at home a thing to envy.

Coleman Silk's big secret—kept from his wife of forty years, from his children, from everyone—is that he's black ("African American" isn't, in Silk's case, quite right), that he's passed as a white man from the day he signed up for the Navy in the second world war. He has another secret too—that, two years after the scandalous close of his career and two years after the death of his wife, he's having an affair with an illiterate thirty-four-year-old cleaning woman, called Faunia Farley, who works at the college. He has received an anonymous, ominous letter saying that "Everyone knows" of his affair, a letter that, as we discover, has been sent in tortured secrecy by the young new chair of Silk's department, Delphine Roux, herself secretly . . .

And so it goes. Some of these secrets are of a wholly different order than others, but in all they bring to mind the importance of big secrets to the modern novel— Rochester's Bertha, Pip's Magwitch, Gatsby's money . . . there's a very long list, including of course a great many famous illicit affairs in addition to Mme. Bovary's. These secrets seem inescapable parts of modern life, inescapable for all of "us" who for whatever reason have been cut loose from our origins and set out to wend our ways towards identity under circumstances of dizzying, bewildering, irresistibly tempting and often damned scary possibility.

For a long time the American take on this trajectory between past and present, this modern pilgrim's progress, was captured in the hopeful (albeit slightly uncomfortable) metaphor of "the melting pot." People from all over came to the United States and were dissolved and reconstituted into a new whole. Where once identity was almost altogether determined by place of birth, caste, class, religion, race—now it would be determined by the activity of the self (and if you were born in the States, a kind of analogous internal emigration and immigration was assumed). Although this was a supremely secular and thoroughly social matter, it was also, as emphatically, an existential one. Where once you were promised a soul's due in the afterlife while you were hobbled on earth with identities which seemed to embrace everything *except* your self, now you could at last live a life that joined self and soul. This was the American adventure.

Milan Kundera has said about Roth that his "nostalgia" for his parents' world—the lost world of the upstanding American--has imparted to his work "not only an aura of tenderness but an entire novelistic background." In Roth's recent books this background has become foreground; and maybe it always was the foreground, that is, the location for the main line of exploration in Roth's work, which is the exploration of the conditions of freedom (not liberation, but freedom) in the American melting pot.

In a book full of subtle and definitive reproach to the currently dominant view of America as a "multicultural" collection of unhappily contiguous nationalisms; and in a book that also, incidentally, makes several bows to Faulkner, Roth invents for Silk a wonderfully diverse, mixed up, miscegenated American lineage: Silk learns from his mother that his family (and his Jersey black community) are "descendants of the Indian from the large Lenape settlement at Indian Fields who married a Swede . . .descendants of the two mulatto brothers brought from the West Indies . . . of the two Dutch sisters come from Holland to become their wives . . . of John Fenwick, an English baronet's son . . . [of Fenwick's daughter], Elizabeth Adams, who married a colored man, Gould . . ."

Silk sees even this past as something to be honored, rather than worshipped—"To hell with that imprisonment!" he says. Instead Silk opts "to pass," chooses in other words the path of radical autonomy that, Roth maintains, *is* the fabulous fate of the American, especially in the modern era. *This* is the hand we've been dealt, and anything else is an evasion and a lie—"As though the battle that is each person's singular battle could somehow be abjured, as though voluntarily one could pick up and leave off being one's self, the characteristic, immutable self in whose behalf the battle is undertaken in the first place."

This "singular battle" is, as I read it, what Roth's fiction has been "about" from the beginning. Not that this singular battle isn't muddled and often made more dangerous by one's own hangups, which are fairly likely to include ethnicity, family, the works, and about which Roth has written with humor and fire and really like no one else. And not that this singular battle can be waged in exile from the hangups of the people around you, to which Roth has also paid a lot of attention. But the essential step to maturity, Roth seems to say right from the start, lies in accepting the radical autonomy that, in modern America, *is* the way we live, and that anyway is ultimately and inescapably the ground we stand on in the existential "battle" of being. In *The Human Stain*, through Coleman and Faunia's relationship, Roth delicately, I am tempted to say sweetly shows the purpose of the battle, if I can put it this way, to be the affirmation or better the realization of being, of being pure and simple, the Humanist's "goal" for the examined life. And if that seems paradoxically unintellectual, it's no more paradoxical than, as Montaigne says, that you need a good deal of knowledge and in particular self-knowledge to understand that you don't know anything.

The last third of the novel occupies itself less with Coleman and Faunia than with the imagination—this is, after all, a Zuckerman novel. I want, in closing, to say two things about Zuckerman's imagining. First, that it is rendered, sentence by sentence, in an absolutely beautiful American prose—vulgar and sacred, utterly colloquial (no one has a better ear for talk than Roth) and gracefully intellectual, mundane and eloquent, slapstick and high-toned, ethnic and "standard," street smart and book wise. A prose of great verve, intelligence, and suppleness, it's precisely the melting pot become writing—which, in Roth's hands anyway, is just a great pleasure to read. The second point I want to make has to do with "what happens," in Zuckerman's words, "when you write books," with Zuckerman as author. "There's not just something that drives you to find out everything," Zuckerman says, but "something begins putting everything in your path. There is suddenly no such thing as a back road that doesn't lead headlong into your obsession."

In *The Human Stain* Zuckerman doesn't rant, rave, and rage, and he doesn't stumble into too many wacky situations. But he's still driven by his writerly obsession, he still can't let things go when he thinks, as he does when everyone else is comfortable to close the book on Coleman and Faunia's story, that that just "would not suffice. Too much truth was still concealed." Zuckerman goes on to say "there really is no bottom to what is not known. The truth about us is endless. As are the lies." But nonetheless, even believing that what there is to say about us is endless, nonetheless—in the search for this slippery, *human* truth--Zuckerman continues to violate decorum, to drive down the dangerous back roads, to do things no sane person would dream of doing in real life. So it is *through imagination* that, in a world of radical autonomy, we seek truth: this is the thing, this obsessiveness, that Zuckerman holds in reverence. *The Human Stain* suggests that this might be last of Zuckerman, which maybe sharpens one's appreciation of Zuckerman's obsessiveness as an especially apt and daring form of sustained moral meditation. From *that* point of view alone, we are going to be a lot poorer if, in fact, Zuckerman is about to be retired.

PHILIP ROTH'S *NEMESIS* : *An Evening at YIVO* (May 18, 2011)

I've organized my talk around four questions:

1. How does *Nemesis* fit into the body of Philip Roth's work?

Roth has gone a long way toward answering this question. On the page preceding the title page of *Nemesis,* he lays out a neat Lynean classification of his many novels. At the top are listed the Zuckerman books, beginning with his great novella *The Ghost Writer* and ending with *The Human Stain* and *Exit Ghost;* and towards the bottom is a new grouping, now titled *Nemeses,* and including *Everyman, The Humbling,* and of course *Nemesis.* There's a kind of reversal of thematic focus in Roth's classification system as you go from top to bottom: at the top are the books about the, frequently extremely funny, quarrel between the second and the first generations, books about choice and radical autonomy in the everything-goes US of A; but starting with *American Pastoral* increasingly you come across books about living out what you don't and can't choose—the books visited by Nemesis. Roth emphasizes this shift by giving *The Human Stain,* for example, an epigraph from *Oedipus the King,* and

RECOLLECTIONS, REVERIES, REFLECTIONS

now classifying his recent works under the name of the most vengeful Greek goddess, a merciless and implacable enemy of human choice.

I should say a word more about Roth's generations. In one of those odd coincidences, it so happens that a student in one of the first classes I ever taught—Freshman English at Stanford—was Jonas Salk's youngest son, Jonathan. He was a good looking, serious, and very able boy. His father, the famous scientist, who also, in 1970, married Picasso's ex-mistress Françoise Gilot, was a poor boy from the Bronx, and went to City College. Jonas' father, Daniel, was an uneducated garment worker of Russian Jewish stock. The three Salk generations nicely represent the world of Roth's fiction, albeit that Roth's people come from Newark and not the Bronx, and even more specifically seem all to have been bred on the Chancellor Street playground. The older Newark generation is a daunting model of upstanding responsibility, men and women without much education but plenty of energy and perseverance and, most of all, unreflective certainty about how to live. Roth's second generation is suckled equally on matzo ball soup and the acid free paper of the Great Books, and soon enough these men find themselves in the capital of hanky panky across the

Hudson, where, reveling in the carnival of existential choice, they cast wistful glances back at the place of origin on Chancellor Street. The third generation is the generation of observers, sometimes taking the role of narrators, like Arnie in *Nemesis* (Zuckerman serves in this role too as he ages, as in *The Human Stain* and *American Pastoral*).

2. How does *Nemesis* reflect the plague narratives?

Avishai[8] has already alluded to Camus' novel, but for me the key book, a very Rothean one, is Boccaccio's *Decameron*. Here are a few quotations from Boccaccio's account of the plague in 14th century Florence:

> "Some say that it descended upon the human race through the influence of the heavenly bodies, others that it was a punishment signifying God's righteous anger at our iniquitous way of life . . . In the face of its onrush, all the wisdom and ingenuity of man were unavailing."

> "Large numbers of men and women abandoned their city . . . and headed for the countryside . . . It was as though they imagined that the wrath of God . . . would only be aroused against those who found themselves within the city walls . . ."

---

8 Bernard Avishai, another of the evening's panelists.

"Of the people who held these various opinions [on how to avoid the plague], not all of them died. Nor did they all survive."

3. What should Bucky have done?

Bucky is a shortish, extremely myopic, superbly athletic man of 23, earnest, reliable, diligent, and an orphan. Raised by his maternal grandfather to understand "that a man's every endeavor was imbued with responsibility," he tries in an almost pedantic way to learn where, under the circumstances, his responsibility lies. What should guide him? Where is he to find answers to the questions asked of him by Mr. Michaels, the father of the first boy from the playground to die of polio:

> "Where is the sense in life?"
> "Where are the scales of justice?"
> "Why does tragedy always strike down the people who least deserve it?"

To each of these questions Bucky responds: "I don't know the answer." But he must have an answer, he becomes obsessed with finding an answer. The trouble is that all the advice he receives—from the example of his grandfather; from his soon-to-be-fiancée's father, Dr. Steinberg; from his fiancée

Marcia—somehow doesn't help. So when he makes his first fateful choice—to leave Newark for the mountains—he says yes to Marcia without having intended to, without having decided to: "he startled himself . . . by what he'd just agreed to." For us as readers this choice is opaque, as though we were reading a parable; it is an act without adequate explanation, an act without sufficient interiority. How can we make sense of it? We can look, perhaps, at Bucky's love of diving. In a wonderful moment shortly after he arrives in the Poconos, Bucky goes out alone to the camp's high board. He has to dive without his glasses, so he really cannot see, and when he dives he can longer feel the earth under his feet.

> He filled his lungs with the harmless
> clean air of the Pocono Mountains, then
> bounded three steps forward, took off,
> and, in control of every inch of his body
> throughout the blind flight, did a simple
> swan dive into the water . . .

This is the condition he loves best, free of all external constraint, blind and suspended in the air but: "in control of every inch of his body." The Bucky whom we know as Mr. Cantor, the young

RECOLLECTIONS, REVERIES, REFLECTIONS

man of the first third of the novel, seems admirably in control, already a full-fledged adult, a self-aware actor in life. But the man we come to know as Bucky is beleaguered by obligations he can't quite embrace as his own: raised to fulfill every responsibility, he cannot distinguish among duties, and be himself. When he chooses to quit the playground, therefore, it seems to him he has not chosen: he speaks without intending to, as if someone or something other than himself uttered words for him.

4.   How much does it matter that Arnie Mesnikoff is the story's narrator?

Well, the person who chooses Bucky's words for him is, literally, the Chancellor playground boy and polio victim Arnie Mesnikoff. Arnie doesn't identify himself as the narrator until we're over a hundred pages into the book, and for two thirds of the novel we don't give him a lot of thought. He is never-theless a fastidious raconteur, with an affection for slightly archaic turns of phrase: "one of the boys would rush up unbidden," he says; or: "[he] already knew many of us who habituated the playground"; or: "the driveway where they were congregated." Arnie's diction and syntax seem completely appro-priate to the 1940s America of which he is, here, the bard. The narrative voice, the narrative, and the narrative's protagonist all seem made of one lexicon, all seem to evoke a simpler and nobler America.

Until, that is, Bucky himself is struck with polio and Arnie as the voice of a humane common sense shows himself incapable of understanding either Bucky's dilemma or Bucky's choices. When Bucky tells Arnie that *he* was the poisoned arrow of a vindictive God, that *he* was polio, Arnie is horrified—because, despite the crippling results of his polio, Arnie has married and had children and lived something close to the life he might have lived had he never contracted polio. He tries to persuade Bucky that, even if he had been a carrier of polio, which is far from certain, he was an unsuspecting carrier, and so could not bear any responsibility for the plague. This is like telling Oedipus that, yes, he did kill his father and sleep with his mother, but since he didn't mean it, hey, what was the problem?

Where in the first two sections of the novel Arnie narrates without intruding, in the third and final section he can't allow the story to speak for itself: now he has to interpret and, more, argue. Like Marcia, he finds Arnie's trenchant judgment of God ridiculous—Bucky, he says, exhibits "the hubris of fantastical, childish religious interpretation." He is equally aghast at Bucky's inability to leave impossible theological questions alone: "this maniac of why," he calls him. Marcia and Arnie are members of the church of common sense: to them Bucky's having contracted polio, or maybe even having passed it on to others, is a piece of bad luck, without attribution or meaning. Yes, it is awful; yes, it is hard to bear; but they believe love can counterbalance all of that. It's not something that requires you to pluck your eyes out.

But that's not at all how it looks to Bucky. Roth's epigraph from *Oedipus the King* is about how unspeakable acts can be purified. And in classical Greece there *is* a way: even Oedipus attracts pity, and in the end his ordeal, blind and in exile, magnifies human being. But how can Bucky cleanse himself? There is only one way: he must renounce Marcia, or, put differently, he must set Marcia free. Arnie misunderstands Bucky's act as the consequence of polio having "irreparably damaged his assurance as a virile man." But to Bucky it's the other way around: had he not renounced Marcia, he would have lost his manhood.

In the opening of *Winesburg, Ohio*, a book I know Roth admires, Sherwood Anderson says of the questing characters in that interconnected set of stories that they are "grotesques," and that the collection is best understood as "The Book of the Grotesque." You might say of Anderson's characters that they too are "maniacs of why," and it is true that these kind of people, fixated on meaning, relentlessly themselves, gripped to mania by one truth, are grotesque. In the great Greek tragedies, however, these grotesques, victims of horrible fates every bit as capricious as polio, achieve through their suffering a kind of glory. They do not reject God, and they do not slough off their admonishment as bad luck; but neither do they truckle under. Instead, by inhabiting, as it were, the caprice of Fate, they realize their irreducible singularity, as does Bucky.

Arnie, who says Bucky "has the aura of ineradicable failure," nevertheless does catch faint glimpses of how Bucky might appear if appreciated from a different point of view, which perhaps explains why he ends his narrative with a glorious if ironic portrait of Bucky engaged in that quintessentially Greek act of grace, the throwing of the javelin.

LETTER TO
LOUISE GLUCK

I n the Chatham Bookstore, in the mountains, I found your *Poems 1962-2012*. We lugged the volume (heavy as a Belgian cobblestone) to the pricey cheese store, and then the pub. By the time we drove home, mist had settled on the tops of the hills. The headlights at first lit a path for us, oddly demarcated trees, as in the shadows of an Edward Hopper painting, distant houses with a single light in one window, pulsing yellow roadlines, but then, abruptly, on the hilltops, everything shone a dense, blinding white, as though we had stumbled onto the nuclear threshold of heaven. We fell to earth each time down the familiar black road: I don't know what I want from you, or have ever wanted from you, but I have come back for it now that we have grown old together.

I looked first, to see where you had arrived, at "A Village Life" on page 625, the very last poem in the collection, and from there followed the trail back home like Hansel and Grethel. *Their* story begins with famine: did that give you any pause? Because that isn't the way things are usually paid for in your poems, it's not money that passes hands. The folk tales are humble stories of poverty, there isn't enough food, and the mother—and, as I'm sure you know, it's the *mother* and not the step-mother; the step-mother was forced on Jacob and Wilhelm by their nervous publishers—the nameless mother and father face one of those desperate choices with which we are by now horribly familiar, if only from the images on the evening news, a century of proliferating Sophie's choices . . . them or us, you or me?

I had dinner with Claude Lanzmann many years ago, after *Shoah* had opened in all the theaters. The conversation somehow turned to killing. "The essence of being human," he said, "is that I am willing to kill you." He didn't mean, if he had to choose; he didn't mean, if he were threatened. No, he meant, *before* he was threatened. He meant that, only in choosing yourself over others, the sign of which is your willingness to kill, only by means of that choice do you become fully individual as a human being, *your*-self.

I didn't buy it, and I don't buy it, but I am suspicious of my recoil at the idea, and it troubles me to think that, to read your work, that is, properly, I ought not to recoil.

By the way, the book I had brought with me to the mountains was Steven Weinberg's *To Explain the World: The Discovery of Modern Science*. Weinberg, a Nobel Prize winner and by all accounts the greatest living physicist, writes with that spare, unequivocal authority of the scientists, and here he wants to track and uncover how science, as a way of knowing, came about. At the beginning, he says, by which he means in classical Greece, knowledge took the form of poetry. He defines poetry as "language chosen for aesthetic effect, rather than in an attempt to say clearly what one actually believes to be true."

(Are you laughing?)

For minds like Weinberg's, which is to say for science, there is only one form of knowledge, and that comes from "using proposed theories to draw more or less precise conclusions that can be tested by observation." That's it: that's the only way to discover what's actually true.

Whatever you and I may know, or believe we know, by Weinberg's standard we know nothing.

Weinberg says it never occurred to the early Greeks, or to more or less anyone for many centuries after the death of Aristotle, to test by exact observation whether their assertions about nature and the universe could be verified. It never occurred to them, he says, because *"they had never seen it done"* (Weinberg's italics). This fact of intellectual history fascinates Weinberg.

And if we read Weinberg's careful choice of words carefully, we have to say he's right.

He's talking about the path the moon takes around the earth, and the "fact" that it goes round the earth, and at what rate of speed it goes round the earth, not about whether, when full, the moon makes you howl, your area of expertise.

But, to be clear: your world, the world of Homer and the Greek myths, of Moses, Ovid, of theology, of Jacob and Wilhelm Grimm, this is the world before science, before anyone actually knew anything.

In my edition of *Grimm's Fairy Tales*, after Hansel and Grethel have successfully found their way home the first time and the second famine comes, the mother once more argues that "the children must go." The poor father can't resist. Why? Because

"He who says A must say B, likewise, and as he had yielded the first time, he had to do so a second time also."

A law of the human heart.

That's what "A Village Life" is about, is it? As it happens, I was born in a village, a village in the Slovak backwoods, and so, as far as villages go, a pretty good example of the kind, about as drab as the godforsaken spot where poor Emma Bovary finds herself stranded, and not the Thornton Wilder version to which, after much reading, I (and maybe you too) am attracted, you know, the elemental life, birth, childhood, bilberries warm from the sun, skinny dipping in the creek, marriage, work, sweet evenings of love, then loss, pain, the mountains, death,

> The death and uncertainty that await
>   me
> as they await all men, the shadows
>   evaluating me
> because it can take time to destroy a human
>   being,
> the element of suspense
> needs to be preserved—

After a sidewise glance at "all men"[9] (see "Winter Morning"), I have been stuck at those two short lines—

> the element of suspense
> needs to be preserved—

because there is something about them I can't put my finger on . . . but finally I think I understand it has to do with what comes next:

> On Sundays I walk my neighbor's dog
> so she can go to church to pray for her sick
> mother.

The dog waits for me in the doorway.

The dog waits in your neighbor's doorway, I realize, like those caged letters "e" in the preceding lines— element, suspense, needs, and especially, preserved. Then the door opens. He knows you, he doesn't hesitate to quit his little chamber, he runs free, he breathes freely.

---

9 An aside about the occasional appearance of a persona in these poems. Sometimes "the speaker" in these poems is, say, a flower; and sometimes, a character out of mythology. Are these speakers *you*? For the most part—I hope you don't think this is just saucy—I have side-stepped this question. I don't read you as a ventriloquist, and on the occasions when you pose as a ventriloquist, I still don't read you as a ventriloquist.

Whereas you don't know what to expect when the door opens (any more than any of us knows), and all you can rely on, for now, is suspense (it's your neighbor, after all, who has gone to church).

(Tension and release—that was Anna Akhmatova's particular metrical preference too, the amphibrach, a principle for her—and for you?—not only of sound but composition. I have been reading Akhmatova alongside *Poems 1962-2012* (the book of her *Complete Poems* is even heavier than yours); she makes a good companion for your work, it turns out, a comparison and a foil, even though, in contrast to Akhmatova, nothing has happened to you, you've been free of famine or fear of the state, free of terror or enemy bombs . . . (but then, nothing happened to Emily Dickinson, either). "The True [or, Real] Twentieth Century," Akhmatova said, which all the official histories and all the public rhetoric shied clear of, could be found in her work, at once private, inward, closed, and a record (from a certain vantage point, *the* record) of her time. By "The True Twentieth Century" she meant the lived history of totalitarianism and of war in her time, or even more broadly, within the grand sweep of Russian literary tradition, the record of the individual life in the grip of (an unremittingly dark) History.

"I have lived for thirty years/Under the wing of death," she wrote in the late nineteen-fifties. I don't know whether she wrote those lines in the Fountain House, where through some perverse but inspired bureaucratic policy the Russian State allowed her to live, in the grandest palace in Petersburg, suitable for the grandest poet, but in the smallest, barest of rooms, because she was unreliable and, even when silenced, eloquent—and anyway it was good to have her close at hand, should there be need to find her and haul her off for execution.

"In the terrible years of the Yezhov terror," Akhmatova writes to introduce her great sequence "Requiem," "I spent seventeen months in the prison lines of Leningrad. Once, someone 'recognized' me. Then a woman with bluish lips standing behind me, who, of course, had never heard me called by name before, woke up from the stupor to which everyone had succumbed and whispered in my ear (everyone spoke in whispers there):

'Can you describe this?'
And I answered: 'Yes, I can.'
Then something that looked like a smile·
passed over what had once been her face."

The role of the poet, then, the *national* poet, one whose name is known even, or especially, to those queuing outside the prison gates, is *to give voice*. It is a complication that this role must be filled by a living human being, a complication that I take to be the subject of more or less everything Akhmatova wrote.

The death that looms over Akhmatova is death in the form of killing, usually at the hands of the State; in our twentieth century (spent on Long Island, say, or in Cambridge, Mass.) people die on account of having lived.

Can you describe that?
Yes, you can.)

Well, at least the neighbor's dog gets you out of the house and, as you say, to notice some things, the monarda, and to neglect others, "the ratio/ of the body to the void shifting."

"Ratio" is a cold word of impersonal measurement, the cold mind applied to the living body, as in Blake's depiction of Newton, and suggests precision of an unsentimental sort, the possibility of exact observation of the disintegrating body as it approaches death, or perhaps of the emotional relationship between that body—being—and nothingness (whereas shifting is what we do with the living body?). Robert Hass, in his essay on Wallace Stevens' "The Emperor of Ice Cream," says "void" is a word from the existentialist 1950s, a word of fashionable misery that enthralled the whole of our set, that is, those of us with a taste for words who were rising out of adolescence at that time; and, insofar as he's right, which he usually is, the word must have enthralled you, too. ("Maybe you have some kind of void syndrome"?)

Ratio.

Ration.

Rational.

Rationale.

Rationalization.

Ratio in its original use, meaning "the faculty of discursive reasoning," is still current, as perhaps you've noticed, in theological discourse, but otherwise, according to the OED, we're talking about "a proportional relationship between things not precisely measurable," for which there's an example cited from Smollett's *Peregrine Pickle*: "You must allow that passion acts upon the human mind, in a ratio compounded of the acuteness of sense, and constitutional heat."

Perhaps you wanted "ratio" to block the path— for us and for you—to sentimental indulgence, or any form of rationalization. (Somewhere in Philip Roth's novels: "Everyone is immortal, until they die.") But this has to do with the body, the torn rotator cuff, spidery veins, gnarled fingers, sagging breasts and ass, shortness of breath and haste of urination, "things not precisely measurable" . . .

so much waist as she cannot embrace

My mountain belly and my rocky face.

Ben Jonson was forty-seven when he wrote those lines: for you and me, years of vigor and youthfulness, when it was still possible to look in the mirror.

After a lifetime of irritated, and inspired, complaint about the plain fact of the matter, that soul and mind are mired in body (would you put it that way?), now, shifting toward the void, all there is to die for is body.

A woman's body.
Even so, you don't seem to want to claim it.
Is it *your* body?
"*The* body, *the* void . . ."

(Already in the poems of the young Akhmatova, in her first book, *Evening*, a kind of double narrative imposes itself or emerges, at once almost opaquely personal, possessive, interior, and at the same time *national*, by which I mean the personal life made public, resonant of the national life, placed within the discourse of tradition, and so uniquely representative.

No hint of pain oppresses my breast,

> If you like, look into my eyes.
> But I don't like the hour before sunset,
> The wind from the sea and the word: "Leave!"

2.

> . . . And there's my marble double,
> Lying under the ancient maple,
> He has given his face to the waters of
>   the lake,
> And he's listening to the green rustling.

3.

A dark-skinned youth wandered along
    these allees.
By the shores of this lake he yearned,
And a hundred years later we cherish
The rustle of steps, faintly heard.

The dark-skinned youth is Pushkin, who, like Akhmatova, lived at Tsarskoye Selo (the Tsar's Village, near St. Petersburg) when he was young, and where, in 1911, the just-married Akhmatova wrote these lines while her (first) husband, the poet Nikolay Gumilyov, was off on one of his many journeys, this one to Abyssinia. She is not a happily married young woman (she was never, then or later, happy never mind lucky in love), the language is terse, "edgy": the theme is pain. But the woman suffering is not, as it were, singular; here Akhmatova notices, as if she had stumbled upon him by chance, coming upon him at the end of a path, her "marble double." Her poems from before the First World War often have an uncanny prescience to them, like this one, where she envisions herself already among the (male) literary statuary of Tsarskoye Selo. In any event, her marble double is only one among many Others in the body of her work, persons in whom she finds herself represented, or in whom she glimpses what might have been her/self. She could have been like this one or that one; her fate, as a flesh-and-blood woman, always seems played out in parallel universes. The difference, though, between Akhmatova the poet and her doubles is clarified by her awareness of the presence of Pushkin. It is with Pushkin that she belongs, in whose steps she walks: her doubles live her possible lives as a woman, a lover, a person on a queue outside a prison, but her *life* is writing, and *in* the writing.

In the early poems, written before 1913—the date she chooses, in her masterpiece "Poem Without a Hero," to mark the divide between her youth and innocence in the twilight of the nineteenth century (or, if you prefer, the parturition of the twentieth), and the years after the Fall, in the True Twentieth Century—in the early poems, the Romantic aura of a life among the allees where Pushkin walked veils the full burden of such a life *in the future*. The world has not yet been turned upsidedown.

It's a nice coincidence (if it is a coincidence) that the one time you bring Pushkin into the picture—in "Omens"—you offer a gloss on what it's tempting to call the Parable of the Poet, a parable that's at least in part about the relation between present and future, experience and meaning.

> I rode to meet you: dreams
> like living beings swarmed around me
> and the moon on my right side
> followed me, burning.

> I rode back: everything changed.
> My soul in love was sad
> and the moon on my left side
> trailed me without hope.

> To such endless impressions
> we poets give ourselves absolutely,
> making, in silence, omen of mere event,
> until the world reflects the deepest needs
> of the soul.

(Incidentally, have you ever sat on a horse? In the winter, in the snow?) Experience, Virginia Woolf said, is a flood of impressions, in and of themselves no more than (to use your word) events, meaning, of little consequence. To combat the meaningless flood, Woolf wanted to "transfix" the moment, to nail it to consciousness, consciousness, which need not rush along but, through art, might be made still. More than that, made to reflect the deepest needs of the soul.

Which it turns out are not so mysterious, merely elusive—in life.

How should the poet read her life? As an omen.)

But to return to "the thousand natural shocks/that flesh is heir to." When the teenage Mary Shelley found herself abroad, along with Byron, Shelley, Polidori, and her rapacious half-sister, Claire, trapped indoors on vacation by a stretch of bad summer weather—the bunch of them constituting the human material for an A-grade research library on the topic of desire—in these circumstances, Mary Shelley imagined Frankenstein's Creature stumbling for the very first time upon an image of himself. He has been hidden away in a little hut or shed adjoining the cabin of the DeLaceys , whose beauty and gentleness dazzle him.

> "I had admired the perfect forms of my
> cottagers—their grace, beauty, and delicate
> complexions: but how was I terrified, when
> I viewed myself in a transparent pool! At

first I started back, unable to believe it was
indeed I who was reflected in the mirror;
and when I became fully convinced that
I was in reality the monster that I am, I
was filled with the bitterest sensations of
despondence and mortification. Alas!
I did not yet entirely know the fatal effects
of this miserable deformity."

We're all upset, or worse—aren't we?— by
the dreadful discrepancy between what we feel
ourselves to be and what we see in the mirror, so the
unpalatable truth is that the Creature's miserable
deformity afflicts us all. But the genius of Shelley's
idea of the Creature, a person "born" as an adult,
transforms what for the rest of us is a long, slow
process of recognition into a traumatic flash of
insight. The Creature discovers to his horror the
first time he is able to "see" himself that he is not
only rationality, benevolence, sensibility, but also
Body, and that while his inner self radiates wonder
and feels wonderfully desirable his outer self is
monstrous, repulsive. It takes him a while longer to
grasp the full "fatal effects" of his discovery: that
"he" is not only embodied but that he *is* Body. As
an embodied being he can anticipate being loved

by someone else who might see beyond Body to "Self," or to what he knows as "Self." But he never encounters such a person: others just see his body, and judge him on that basis alone, including the admirable DeLaceys, and his Maker.

And he is no different: he admires the beauty, the complexions of the DeLaceys. He calls the image in the pool "the monster that I am."

Perceiving himself as monstrous, he is "filled with the bitterest sensations of despondence and mortification." (To how many of your poems might that apply?)

I say "he" because we know he is male, but at this point in his life-experience does *he* know it? The Creature is perhaps the only character in literature who might be said to have a non-gendered consciousness. Virginia Woolf's Orlando is man and woman; or man-woman. But the Creature is a being whose awareness, for a time, is absent of gender, precedes gender. How does he know what he is? How *can* he know what he is if he does not know he has a body?

You understand what I'm talking about, I'm sure, because to the very end you are bitter about puberty, as, here, in the middle stanza of "A Village Life":

I'm tense, like a child approaching adolescence.

> Soon it will be decided for certain what
>   you are,
> one thing, a boy or a girl. Not both any
>   longer.
> And the child thinks: I want to have a say
>   in what happens.
> But the child has no say whatsoever.

> When I was a child, I did not foresee this.

When you had crossed that threshold from childhood to adolescence, just far enough to model yourself on the magazines, you were already, as you say in "Summer at the Beach," vividly displeased with your fate as Body: you could not imagine going back, because babies can't think; but you hated the idea of going forward even more, becoming an adult:

> They all had terrible bodies: lax, oily,
>   completely
> committed to being male and female.

(That "completely" teeters at the end of the line as a sad, poignant, final, impossible hanging back before the inescapable "commitment" to gender.)

I am trying to picture that girl on the beach. This must have been a Long Island beach, back in the day, immense stretches of amazingly fine sand; the flat, cold, booming sea; the fierce sun; and the heat.

There are no beaches in Slovakia; but after the Second World War my family settled for a time in Ecuador and, in the summers, we flew from Quito in a commercial propeller aircraft over the Andes to a seaside hotel in Manta, on the Pacific coast. There, like you, I studied the bodies. Then, a year after we had arrived in the U.S., my father bought a Chrysler sedan, and the first thing we did, to celebrate, was drive out to Jones Beach. This would be 1953. I was twelve.

Manta was a cozy, placid resort compared to the vastness of Jones Beach, in the early 1950s a spectacle of public grandeur, with its massive stone restaurants and immaculate parking lots. There was something fierce and daunting, too, about that desert-sized expanse of beach, the sand burning the soles of your feet, the sun grilling your skin. On my first visit, I returned home with my neck, face, back, arms, legs already blistering and unnaturally red.

But you don't even think about going into the water: you sit, "coltish," in the sand, and cover your feet so you can "sustain [the] deception" that you are taller, lankier than in fact you are (more Audrey Hepburn and less Elizabeth Taylor?). You don't move.

That's the key, I guess. You are not racing headlong into the water; you are not playing beach volleyball (though I like that idea); you are not eating a tuna sandwich or a Good Humor bar (are you eating at all?). I imagine that girl, in her fixed pose, as braced against both past and future, the unthinkable infancy and the horrifying post-adolescence. She doesn't move, betting that her composure will not just protect her—because that girl never feels safe—but transport her.

I sat with my legs arranged to resemble
    what I saw in my head, what I believed
        was my true self.

Because it *was* true: when I didn't move I
        was perfect.

That girl thinks she can, through discipline and aesthetic deception, master her fate, and be perfect. The only safety is in perfection. But what threatens her? And: whom does she want to impress?

Boys? Maybe we saw each other at the beach. I don't imagine you would have looked at me, but I would have looked at you. I was furiously studying how to be an American boy, the kind of guy the magazines—*Mademoiselle? Seventeen?*—were getting you ready for (1953 is the year when Sylvia Plath was guest editor at *Mademoiselle*). But unlike you I wasn't doing such a good job (I was never comfortable on any playing field). I knew from my mother about fashion, though, and from your pose would have spotted you as a connoisseur. My mother's house in Slovakia backed onto the estate wall of the Malacky branch of the Counts Palffy, the Hungarian family that ruled Slovakia. She dreamt of marrying a prince, and, when that didn't work out, devoted herself to mastering princely tastes (and dressed me, her only child, like a little prince). She was a seamstress: once she arrived in New York, fantasy and reality beautifully merged for her in the pages of *Vogue*. When she saw something in *Vogue* she especially admired, she'd purchase the pattern, which I guess you could do through the magazine, and make herself the dress or jacket. Barely five feet tall, she was trim, and did not leave the house if she didn't look . . . perfect (read: as in *Vogue*). So I would have recognized what you were up to, and, because at that time I still suffered from nightmares about the War, might have sensed too what was going on underneath the studied pose.

It's your mother who takes you to the beach, your mother but not exactly, as you render her, a maternal figure (my mother wasn't a maternal figure, either). She has wounded you in many ways. Given what is going to happen (and in fact what has already happened) to that girl on the beach, you conclude it would have been better not to have been born (a very classical thought).

It was better [you tell your mother] when
we were
together in one body [,]

when you basked in

the absolute
knowledge of the unborn—

but your mother takes this from you—her first, most brutal theft—at birth ("For My Mother"). Now you have a body all your own, but it's not perfect. Worse, it can be harmed (and can do harm, as Frankenstein's Creature also learns—that's *his* coming-of-age).

(When Akhmatova writes about herself as a girl at the beach—"By the Seaside"—she remembers a tomboyish vagabond, "bold and bad and gay," who buries her yellow dress in the sand so the tramp won't find it, and swims out to the rocks to sunbathe and chat with the gulls—"completely unaware that this—was happiness."

This is a girl whom it's hard to read. The poem, a pivotal poem in the body of her work, is a longish narrative fable, unlike Akhmatova's usual brief lyrics; it was written in 1913 or 1914, but the judgment, sense of loss and foreboding, are, again, eerily prophetic, as though the poem had been written many grueling decades later. (I'm reminded of Wordsworth complaining, in "Tintern Abbey," that now that he's twenty-eight he's lost the vivacity of youth, the vigor and vision of the twenty-three-year-old boy, as he remembers him, who first visited the Wye.) The poem's sunny, distinctively happy Russian childhood seems something of a fiction, for elsewhere Akhmatova insists she "had no rosy childhood/With freckles, teddies and toys . . . And people's voices were not dear to me." We know that when she was five years old her younger sister Rika died of TB, casting what she says was a dark shadow over the whole of her childhood (her mother suffered from TB, her older sister Iya died of it at twenty-seven, and Akhmatova herself was stricken by the disease—but it did not kill her: nothing that killed others, especially those close to her, succeeded in killing her).

And yet, Akhmatova's melancholy realization, already in 1913, that that "bold and bad and gay" girl will never again know happiness in the same full-throated girlish way is completely convincing, and felt in the reading less as regret than as renunciation. Like "Poem Without a Hero," "By the Seaside" layers or ignores the distinction of past and present, recollection and fable. The tenderly rendered vagabond swims as she likes, becomes "fast friends" with the fishermen, and, haughtily convinced she will become the tsaritsa, brushes off the "gray-eyed boy" who brings her white roses and wants to marry her. "What are you," she asks him, "the tsarevich?" Soon, she tells him, "I am going to be the tsaritsa,/What good will a husband be then?" The gypsy woman reads her future:

Soon you'll be merry, rich you will be.

Expect a distinguished guest before Easter.

You will bow to this distinguished guest,

Not with your beauty, not with love,

But with your singular song you'll attract

this guest.

Many men were attracted to Akhmatova by her song. But never the right man. (Maxine Hong Kingston tells of her dead, never-to-be-named aunt who, when she is alone in her half-deserted Chinese village—because most of the men have gone off to the gold mountain (the U.S.)— puzzles over how she can do her hair in just such a way as to attract only one man among those who have remained behind, how to attract only the man she wants to attract and not all the others at the same time. Presumably Akhmatova never mastered this skill.)

As Akhmatova imagines the tsarevich appearing, seduced by her song as forecast, a curious tremor runs through the poem, not unlike what occurs at the ending of Wordsworth's "Tintern Abbey," also a poem, in its own way, about beckoning the tsarevich. Neither Wordsworth nor Akhmatova seems confident about how to bring these poems to a close, both suddenly fearful, to use Akhmatova's language, that once they put the finishing touches on these poems the Muse will never visit them again. In the case of "Tintern Abbey," the poem seems already to have come to an eloquent close when Wordsworth unexpectedly picks up the argument yet again. Over and over he has invoked a kind of perfection of experience—what he once was—and at the same time lamented its loss. Now, over one hundred lines into the poem, he remains nervous or anxious or unsatisfied about whether he can sustain his imaginative vigor. Abruptly, Dorothy appears ("my dearest Friend/My dear, dear Friend"—maybe an instance of protesting too much?). Not yet thirty-years-old, Wordsworth fears the very source of his imaginative engagement with nature, his "inspiration," is drying up. Only the idea that Dorothy will carry on reassures him; only once he has passed the baton to her can he finally let the poem end.

In "By the Seaside" a sister also appears out of the blue—Lena.

> I was almost the same age as my sister,
> And we so much resembled each other,
> That when we were small, our mother
> Had to look at our birthmarks to tell us
> apart.

From childhood my sister couldn't walk . . .
And she was embroidering a shroud.

Unlike Dorothy Wordsworth, always at the service
of her brother, Lena is a skeptical, doubting double,
a drag more than a support, representing doubt and
banality. Lena wants to know:

"Where did you hear the song,
The one that will lure the tsarevich?"
. . . .
Bending down close to her ear,
I whispered to her: "Lena, you know,
I myself made up the song."

But that's not quite right. Throughout her career
Ahkmatova spoke of her poems as unexpected gifts
from unexpected visitations of the Muse. Especially
before 1913, her ambition chooses her role, or, put
differently, the living woman, bold and gay and
intoxicated with freedom, in particular the freedom
to do and be what she likes—the living woman
wilfully selects her vocation. Many decades later, in
"Poem Without a Hero," she is ready to recognize—
though even then, not quite resigned to the idea—
that her gift, her role, has chosen *her*, or, put differ-

ently, that her gift has determined the course of her life. Before 1913, she imagines she can be what she chooses and can live as she likes; after 1913, it is too late, she has to be what she is, and she has to pay the price, too, of being what she is, which is not simply a flesh-and-blood woman but a woman in the role of national poet, fated, no matter what, to give voice.

In imagining herself as the tsaritsa, Akhmatova imagines the woman and the role as beautifully merged in union with the tsarevich, a union that anticipates both an emotional and an aesthetic state of perfect fulfillment, blissful as well as easy to have and to hold. But as I've said, the idea of exposing this fulfillment to the light of day sends a tremor through the poem, as Akhmatova tries to put on the brakes so she doesn't have to anticipate or encounter the future. And so, as the vagabond girl roams the beach, singing her siren's song, she grows drowsy, falls asleep, and wakes to find "an enormous old man, groping about/The deep crevasses in the rocks" where a sailboat has foundered.

> Dark-skinned and sweet, my tsarevich
> Quietly lay and gazed at the sky.
> Those eyes greener than the sea

And darker than our cypress trees—
I saw how they were extinguished . . .
Would that I had been blind from birth.

The tsarevich is dead: what will Akhmatova's life be like now that the tsarevich is dead?)

Summer at the beach, with its Beach Boys soundtrack, its luxurious colors, its excess of pleasure, its flippancy, is for you a grimly ironic setting: not a place of summer fun but rather of primal conflict among the members of the family, as in Grimm's fairy tales. You are by far the most dangerous of the people on the sand: and at the same time the most unsettled.

Unsettled, for example, by "Terrible/storms off the Atlantic" threatening your supposedly safe family circle, "a closed form," as you call it. You and your sister—that is, your living sister; your dead sister, like Akhmatova's, seems to have cast a shadow not only across your childhood, but across these poems, too—anyhow, you and your sister, huddled indoors, "felt safe/meaning we saw the world as dangerous." Of course: if you see things coldly, see things as they are, you will grasp that no matter where you may be, in truth you are always in the life- threatening forest. (This was my mother's line, too, the refrain of the Jewish mother. My father on the other hand overcame every obstacle without bitterness. He was not forbidding, my father, like yours, but charming and incredibly diligent. But no match for my mother.) Your sister is frightened, even within the safe circle, and takes your hand.

> Neither of us could see, yet,
> the cost of any of this.
> But she was frightened, she trusted me.

Later, in another poem set at the seaside, this sister appears again (now the cost begins to come into view).

> When you fall in love, my sister said,
> it's like being struck by lightning.

Which is the sort of thing we expect from this sister, incapable, as you represent her, of deception.

> I reminded her that she was repeating
>   exactly
> our mother's formula, which she and I

had discussed in childhood, because we
  both felt

that what we were looking at in the adults

were the effects not of lightning
but of the electric chair.

When I get to this passage on the trail of your
poems I dread reading further. I know what I am
going to come across down the line. I know I am
going to encounter the poems written when you are
besotted—yes, besotted—with love, and then the
wrenching poems when you are, how to put it? . . .
hurt? . . .

I close the book and go for a walk.

It's a cloudy day in mid-March, intermittent
rain, pale-green leaves, twisted, pushing up through
the earth. (When you think of things growing you are
especially attentive, I notice, to lettuce, so delicate
and tender when the plant first spreads up out of the
soil: perhaps the young leaves awake something sentimental in you. But more on this later.) The clouds
rush along above me: Each of us knows our little
dramas are dwarfed by, and also succored by, our

amazing, incomprehensible astrophysical condition. When I return to my desk, I read:

> Who can say what the world is? The world
> is in flux, therefore
> unreadable, the winds shifting,
> the great plates invisibly shifting and
> changing—

Lightning, rain, constellations . . . Maybe I've read enough? Maybe I'll stop here and take what consolation there is in your black humor, your Anne Sexton-y tone, your gestures of appeasement . . .

(Although Akhmatova kills the tsarevich in "By the Seaside," in truth she can't do without him, or so she imagines. She identifies him with the fulfillment of her fate: how, then, can she do without him? "Poem Without a Hero" seems, on first reading, to be a highly stylized or ritualized, operatic answer to that question, Akhmatova's coming-to-terms with her life as it actually came to pass, without any Romantic projection of fulfillment; but I think on reflection it's better understood as a chastened reconceptualization of it, the tell-tale sign of which is the poem's labyrinth of reference and allusion.

To take some an example from the opening of the

poem, the single epigraph is from
Mozart's *Don Giovanni:*

Di rider finirai
Pria dell' aurora
(You will stop laughing
Before dawn)

Akhmatova begins writing the poem in 1940, at the very lowest point in her life, in the life of her beloved Petersburg, in the life of the Europe-as-artistic-home to which, at such great personal expense, she remained faithful from the very first moment she set pen to paper. The world all around her is in tatters, so many of the people she had loved are dead, she is a writer almost without an audience. Against all that, "Poem Without a Hero" sets *Don Giovanni.*

Then, before the poem proper begins, Akhmatova inserts a brief passage in prose, dated April 8, 1943, Tashkent, where she was sent along with most of Leningrad's writers to get them out of harm's way when the city had become too dangerous to live in. The prose passage is titled "In Place of a

Foreword," and is itself preceded by two epigraphs. The first—

Deus conservat Omnia

(God takes care of everything, the motto on the coat of arms of the Fountain House)—

reaches back across Russia, literally and figuratively, from Tashkent to Petersburg, from her grim exile to the Fountain House as symbol of Petersburg past and present; and the second, the last line of Pushkin's *Eugene Onegin*:

"Some are gone and others are far away,"

a good-bye from the writer to his poem and at the same time a greeting from the writer to his readers, identifies Akhmatova as the heir and living voice of the main line of Russian literary tradition.

So, *Don Giovanni*. The Fountain House, Pushkin.

Akhmatova approaches the poem proper via three formal "dedications," the first of which is

In memory of Vs. K.

that is, Vsevolod Knyazev, a young poet and Officer of the Guard, who killed himself out of love for

Akhmatova's friend and rival, the performer Olga Glebova-Sudeikina, whom Akhmatova casts in a leading role in "Poem Without a Hero." It's impossible not to think Akhmatova also had in mind her first husband, Nikolai Gumilyov, who attempted suicide more than once (the first time when Akhmatova was sixteen), because Akhmatova did not return *his l*ove. In *Hope Abandoned* Nadezhda Mandelstam says the invocation of Knyazev should also be understood to call up Nadezhda Mandelstam's husband, Akhmatova's close friend (and perhaps lover?) Osip Mandelstam, the great poetic figure of the early Bolshevik era, who, like Gumilyov, perished in Stalin's camps.

This dedication—like the second, to Olga Glebova-Sudeikina; and the third, to Isaiah Berlin, who visited Akhmatova in late 1945 and early 1946 (Akhmatova ascribed to their meeting the beginning of the Cold War)—much more than the oblique earlier reference to Tsarskoye Selo, establishes the central trope for the poem, mixing Akhmatova's "private" life (by the time she began "Poem Without a Hero" she cannot have thought there could any longer be anything "private" about her life) and myth, while at the same time anchoring myth (and history and artistic tradition) in the everyday, "private" life.

These dedications set the scene for the poem, at last, to begin. It is New Year's eve and Akhmatova is visited by a bevy of masquers, ghosts of her youth in the years before 1913, who arrive in appropriately allusive costumes:

> This one is Faust, that one Don Juan,
> Dapertutto, Jokanaan,
> And the most modest one—the
> northern Glahn
> Or the murderer Dorian Gray . . .

And that's how the poem, which Akhmatova calls a "tryptich," proceeds. The first and by far the longest part is devoted to the years before 1913, and the ghosts of the pre-twentieth century past; the second, turning everything that came before upside down, to the appalling years after; and the epilogue to Petersburg, Petersburg under siege during the Second World War, the physical city where individuals starve, suffer, and die, and Petersburg the living symbol of Akhmatova's Russia, which is to say the city of Pushkin and Dostoevsky, of words and songs.

Akhmatova draws a very sharp line between her world up to 1913, and her world after. Up to 1913 young men had their heads so stuffed with vainglory that suicide on account of unrequited love looked to be as noble as, say, immolation following the loss of a battle, a grand gesture, heroic, immortalizing. They were intoxicated with the Byronic image of themselves standing (dressed to the nines in military splendor) at the edge of a deep, dark ravine—the deeper and darker the better—defying the gods. After 1913, Akhmatova finds all this embarrassing and silly; she doesn't want to look back on the girl she was then.

Before 1913 Akhmatova lived heedlessly, doing as she liked, and writing about what she liked, for the most part her intimate life as a woman. After 1913 Akhmatova found herself increasingly marked out as a historical personage.

Writing of Knyazev at the close of the first part of "Poem Without a Hero," Akhmatova says her goodbye to the world of her youth:

> *Of all the ways for a poet to die,*
> *Foolish boy: He chose this one—*
> *He could not bear the first insult,*
> *He did not know on what threshold*
> *He stood and what road*
> *Spread its view before him . . .*

Akhmatova, too, could not bear the first insult, but she did not die (nor did you); she did not die after the second, the third, the subsequent decades of insults . . . Instead she says she has been "left alive" (as you have been). Now, fifty years old, ill, after all her bitter losses facing yet more suffering and loss, at this extremely dark moment in her life, she is surprised by remarkable snatches of verse—which, she says, just "came" to her, unexpected visitations, she says, of her Muse. Eventually she arrives at the conviction that, composed into dramatic form, these verses will "describe" the true twentieth century, and "solve the riddle of [her] life" (the same riddle you want to solve).

In the event, of course, Akhmatova's solution isn't quite what anyone might have expected. Instead of a solution or "answer" Akhmatova drives the reader to the place she has made out of reference and allusion, "the place where," she says in one of her footnotes to "Poem Without a Hero," "in the readers' imagination, the entire poetic work was born":

> To the darkness under Manfred's fir tree,
>   And to the shore where lifeless Shelley,
>   Staring straight up at the heavens,

lies—
And all the world's skylarks
  Burst the abyss of the ether,
    And George holds the torch.

Akhmatova evades and overcomes her personal, political, temporal dire circumstances by a kind of imaginary resettlement among the timeless allees of artistic tradition. The poem is not exactly an answer as much as it is, to use one of Wordsworth's favorite phrases, a "dwelling place": instead of rewriting the ending of "By the Seaside" to reunite her with the tsarevich after so much tragic experience, Akhmatova makes a home for herself and the tsarevich out of memory and allusion. This "dwelling place" is, for Akhmatova, the "real" or "true" Petersburg, a place-in-the-mind the presiding genius of which, the representative figure for how artifice renders life, is . . . Don Juan (the poem alludes to Mozart's opera, Moliere's play as produced by Vsevolod Meyerhold, Pushkin's drama about Don Juan, "The Stone Guest," in which the phrase "the stone steps of the Commander" appears, a phrase that enters Russian writing to indicate the approach of a sinister fate and which Akhmatova employs while also making reference to Alexander Blok's poem "The Commander's Steps"; and, finally, and not least, Byron's *Don Juan*).

The situation as Akhmatova faces it in 1940 is that the real twentieth century has so inverted authority, elevating cruelty and debasing even the simplest truth, that what was once the nourishing root of personal and national identity—the artistic culture—has been systematically eradicated, almost wiped out entirely, and only survives, as in *Fahrenheit 451*, in memorized verses treasured by no more than a handful of readers and writers, somehow not yet dead. Even *she* is dislodged from her place; even *she* doesn't know where she belongs.

And so, over the span of twenty years, she rebuilds—and she is quite thorough: she peoples the place and gives it words, plots, streets, lovers, music, dance, drama, clothes, masks, tribulations, wine, poison, death . . . it takes her twenty years but in the end she succeeds in making a home for herself and the tsarevich.

The place is wonderfully cosmopolitan, the achievement . . . the right word really is "heroic."

And yet, as someone born in a small country plagued for centuries by the careless egotism of the "great," I admit I am not altogether enchanted by it.

I don't know about you, but although I love Byron's *Don Juan* and Byron's fabulous letters, I can barely bring myself to read the ridiculous *Manfred*. And yet (!) Akhmatova locates the origin of her poem—and by implication the origin of poetry altogether—in the soil under Manfred's fir tree.

I can just imagine what Svejk or one of Bohumil Hrabal's pub goers would say.

There is an inescapably melodramatic, even histrionic dimension to the city-scape Akhmatova establishes in "Poem Without a Hero." I don't think there's too much of Dostoevsky's feverish national mysticism in Akhmatova, but she feels what happens to Russia in her person, so that, for example, she tells us the great shock of her youth was the destruction of the Russian fleet by the Japanese at Tsushima. She never seriously entertained the idea of fleeing Stalin's Russia, and for many years disdained those of her friends who had emigrated. The trouble is that identifying yourself with the soil of your native land can be, like hatred, dangerous for one's moral well-being, no less for Akhmatova than anyone else. Mother Russia! This Romantic vein of emotion becomes revolutionary in Shelley and maybe *Manfred*, but in every case it's bombastic and grandiose: and in my part of the Slavic world this grandiosity, men thinking they can keep company with gods, has always spelled trouble.

The Byron of *Don Juan*, thankfully, is a pretty far cry from the suicidal propagandist of *Manfred*. Byron's world-view in *Don Juan* is aristocratic (hock and soda water) and arrogant but without cant or gall, witty, compassionate not out of principle or ideology but simply genuine fellow-feeling, sybaritic, exhausting every appetite, including of course every sexual appetite (but maybe, like Tom Jones, sexist without being exploitative?), patriarchal in politics, but, like the views of Ford Madox Ford's hero Christopher Tietjens, so conservative as to be mistaken for socialism. In the war between Classic and Romantic Byron disdainfully identified himself with the Classic—did he ever have a kind word for Wordsworth?—but his themes, affections, and politics place him in the other camp, obviously in *Manfred* but equally in *Don Juan*.

Akhmatova also has a foot in both camps, and belongs in the haughty company she has chosen. On her stage Sudeikina is an actress, a dancer, a vamp, an oracle, symbol of the age . . . she calls her her double, but only in the form of a double does

Akhmatova inhabit the hallucinatory old world she has summoned on New Year's Eve. Instead she looks on her old life "As if from a tower" or, in a great image, as if she were "the rime pressing against the windowpane." All of her actors are dead: she has survived them all. They are part of her, but she is not part of them. They died while still playing in the masque: she, on the other hand, has been left alive. The poem opens in the days of her youth, which Akhmatova conveys as a stylized melodrama, each player in costume; the poem ends in Petersburg, where bombs are falling. The artifice that she loves, and that is every writer's home, is not however life: no one can have learned this simple truth more thoroughly or through more searing experience than Akhmatova. That's the solution to the riddle of her life.)

(Just so you know, to make sense of the thicket of your poems, I worked up a kind of spread-sheet of various, ostensibly helpful, thematic categories. Which one do you think got the most entries? That's right: "Things Will Turn Out Badly."

Which is why I am sick of you.
Do you always have to complain?
Trauma shmauma.

How frail are you, anyway, or have you
   ever been?
Frail, touchy, oh-so-sensitive.
"Touch her, and she bleeds" doesn't come
   close:
You bleed no matter what, no touch
   necessary.
Haven't you outlived most of the competition?
A frail woman can be a very manipulative.
Bitch.)

The tsarevich reigns in Akhmatova's operatic city, the city of artifice, but there is no Tsarskoye Selo, with its allee of statues, in your life. When you look back, you don't find Pierrot or Don Juan.

Amazingly, I can look back
fifty years. And there, at the end of the
gaze,
a human being already entirely recogniz-
able,
the hands clutched in the lap, the eyes
staring into the future with the combined
terror and hopelessness of a soul expecting
annihilation.

The poem ("Birthday") looks back to look forward—
"As the future ripens in the past," Akhmatova writes,
"So the past rots in the future." The "bold and bad
and gay" girl at the seaside makes the mistake of
thinking her siren's song will master time; the girl at
the end of the gaze makes the mistake of thinking
she knows the meaning of annihilation. The fate of
the girl at the seaside is turned head-over-heels not
on account of something she has done or failed to
do, but because in every life things happen. Later,
when Akhmatova looks back, she nevertheless faults
the girl for having blithely forgotten that, yes, you
can sail on the waves, but you can also founder on
the rocks. The bold girl at the seaside is overcome by
history, which Akhmatova both registers as reality
and resists by means of her city of reference and
allusion. That's the story of the first half of the
twentieth century, what used to be called "a European
education," meaning an education in what a human
being is capable of, and must be capable of, in the
face of extremity. The story of the second half of
the century, your story, is the story of an American
family, but in your rendering it is a story with classic
dimensions, something like an American tragedy
or home epic (George Eliot's phrase for the novel).
When you write about your mother, your father

you write about the gods; when you write about the gods, you write about your mother, your father. I like especially your poems about Persephone.

The myth of Persephone has everything: love, sex, death, rebirth, betrayal, politics, home and exile, plenty and famine, light and darkness, heaven and hell, illusion and reality . . . all grounded in the relations of mothers and daughters, daughters and lovers, mothers and the lovers of their daughters. You offer two versions of the myth: in the first, Persephone is abducted, and the focus is on Persephone, on being a girl, on being a girl who is "taken," on being a girl who is taken by a demon lover. This Persephone is in a kind of daze, maybe a sex-daze, just awakening to what has happened to her, and to the meaning of her life. You call the poem "Persephone the Wanderer," so the dominant meaning is that she is neither one thing nor another, neither child nor woman, neither at home nor in exile, neither in love (is she afflicted by the Stockholm syndrome?) nor enraged, neither alive nor dead. Demeter is the earth, and in your poems earth is bondage, our inescapable condition. Like Persephone, we could be in heaven, or we could be in hell, but we are on earth:

You must ask yourself
where is it snowing?

. . . .

It is snowing on earth; the cold wind says.

And what is earth? Persephone does not know that
much about earth.

She does know the earth
is run by mothers, this much
is certain,

—mothers, who universally are powerful, dangerous,
—vindictive.

Regarding

incarceration, [Persephone] believes

she has been a prisoner since she has been
a daughter.

You save the main question of the poem for last:

What will you do
when it is your turn in the field with the god?

Well, we know the answer, don't we, because there really isn't any choice, girls are there to be taken, that's what it means to live bound to earth.

The second version, which you also call "Persephone the Wanderer," focuses on Demeter, so, as you say, "the problems of sexuality need not/ trouble us here." Looked at from the mother's point of view, what problems do trouble us? The problems of being, in particular of physical being. "The child's opinion," you say, "is/she has always existed," but the mother knows better. The mother thinks: "*I remember when you didn't exist.*" Of what is that a memory? Does the mother remember a void: existence/nonexistence? Demeter, in your account, grieves over the death of her daughter, but also, much more fundamentally, blames her daughter. Demeter asks: "*what are you doing outside my body?*" The mother's body—earth—is all there is.

> the daughter's body
> doesn't exist, except
> as a branch of the mother's body
> that needs to be
> reattached at any cost.

When Persephone is reunited with her mother, the earth, and spring returns,

> You must ask yourself:
> are the flowers real? If
>
> Persephone "returns" there will be
> one of two reasons:
>
> either she was not dead or
> she is being used
> to support a fiction—

the fiction of eternal renewal, of eternal life. If Persephone's return is a fiction, then the flowers are not real. But "the idiot yellow flowers" are not only real, they are the only reality. Eternal life is a fiction: there is no heaven, and there is no hell, there is only earth. Earth contains qualities both of heaven and of hell.

Another unpalatable truth?

The girl at the end of the gaze, in "Birthday," is traumatized by *being* and expects the worst. But she is a child and has no idea what the worst might be.

All the defenses, the spiritual rigidity, the
  insistent
unmasking of the ordinary to reveal the
  tragic,
were actually innocence of the world.

The annihilation we expect is nothing, just foolish-
ness, compared to what actually happens.

death cannot harm me
more than you have harmed me,
my beloved life. ("October")

The dwelling place you choose, in contrast to
Akhmatova, is a village in the mountains. You are
alone there, although there's the neighbor and her
dog; alone, no mother, no father, no lover, and the
archetypes, the symbols and myths, no longer signify:

the moon is hanging over the earth,
meaningless but full of messages.
It's dead, it's always been dead,
but it pretends to be something else,
burning like a star, and convincingly, so
that you feel sometimes
it could actually make something grow on
earth.

Unlike the two of us, my father was a village boy all his life; he had learned the habits of husbandry early, and ironed his underwear up to the last day before his death. He kept an enormous drawer packed with brilliantly white, meticulously folded Jockey undershirts and underpants. The thousand dollars in hundred dollar bills could always be found in a plain envelope under his socks; and then he made certain there should be two of everything, just in case, in the pantry. He lived, that is, like Conrad's Marlow, though without introspection, by sticking to his routines in what, despite how shallow it sounds, I think is correctly named the present, all of which I attribute to his being a village boy. He of course knew all about growing things, unlike me, a city boy. All the women I have loved, mind you, have had a green thumb, and a vocabulary precise with the names of flowers and soils and angles of the sun. I have managed to grow a few vegetables (though never lettuce), once giant kohlrabi from seeds my cousin gave me in my hometown in Slovakia. That was in a garden in Chalkwell in Essex, on a high ridge overlooking the Thames. In my garden now on the north shore of Long Island the trees hang over the soil, things don't get enough light, the tomatoes are always late. I can just about manage the basil and rosemary, the sage, dill, and thyme. The main thing about being a village boy, in my father's case, was that he did not, like you, live in suspense, even at the end. He didn't expect the moon would make things grow.

In "A Village Life" you don't let us wait too long, though, for the sun to rise, the sun that does make things grow, and allows you this for a last line:

On market days, I go to the market with my lettuces.

So: the simplest truths are the most telling.

Since I was reading from the very end of your volume back to the beginning, it took me some time after reading that last line—both of your poem and of your book—before I came to "Baskets" in *The Triumph of Achilles*, written quarter century earlier.

"Baskets"

1.
It is a good thing,
in the marketplace
the old woman trying to decide
among the lettuces,
impartial, weighing the heads,

examining
the outer leaves, even
sniffing them to catch
the scent of the earth
of which, on one head,
some trace remains—not
the substance but
the residue—so
she prefers it to
the other, more
estranged heads, it
being freshest: nodding
briskly at the vendor's wife,
she makes this preference known,
an old woman, yet
vigorous in judgment.

2.
The circle of the world—
in its midst, a dog
sits at the edge of the fountain.
The children playing there,
coming and going from the village,
pause to greet him, the impulsive
losing interest in play,
in the little village of sticks

adorned with blue fragments of pottery;
they squat beside the dog
who stretches in the hot dust:
arrows of sunlight
dance around him.
Now, in the field beyond,
some great event is ending.
In twos and threes, boldly
swinging their shirts,
the athletes stroll away, scattering
red and blue, blue and dazzling purple
over the plain ground,
over the trivial surface.

3.
Lord, who gave me
my solitude, I watch
the sun descending
in the marketplace
the stalls empty, the remaining children
bicker at the fountain—
But even at night, when it can't be seen,
the flame of the sun
still heats the pavements.
That's why, on earth,
so much life's sprung up,

because the sun maintains
steady warmth at its periphery.
Does this suggest your meaning:
that the game resumes
in the dust beneath
the infant god of the fountain;
there is nothing fixed
there is no assurance of death—

4.
I take my basket to the brazen market,
to the gathering place.
I ask you, how much beauty
can a person bear? It is
heavier than ugliness, even the burden
of emptiness is nothing beside it.
Crates of eggs, papaya, sacks of yellow
lemons—
I am not a strong woman. It isn't easy
to want so much, to walk
with such a heavy basket, either
bent reed, or willow.

THE EXPLAINING NARRATIVES OF ROBERT HASS

Men must endure

Their going hence, even as their coming hither:

Ripeness is all.

–Shakespeare, *King Lear*

"In the twenties a friend is a world"

–Robert Hass, "Those Who Die In
Their Twenties"

On March 1, 1966 Robert Hass and I were
having coffee and pie at an all-night diner
in Palo Alto. We had come from some Stanford
graduate student party, and, although it was two in

the morning, neither of us—Bob in particular[10]—
was ready to go home. As he sipped his coffee, Bob
told me he had made a pact with himself that if he
had not written a novel by the time he was twenty-
five, he would take his life. He had not written a
novel, and that day, he told me, was his twenty-fifth
birthday.

All these years later it strikes me that maybe
the sudden exposure of how little I truly knew of
the close friend sitting across from me, someone I
wholly believed I knew well, frightened me, and so
I dismissed the idea that he might take his life (and,
thankfully, he didn't). I wondered instead about what
gave Bob the idea, and the ambition, to become a
novelist. Because although I knew he loved stories,
I wasn't at all surprised that Bob hadn't written a
novel.

Stanford in those electric years, like Berkeley,
was inflamed with protest, revolutionary talk,
euphoria. I was editor of a rabblerousing newsletter
for graduate students that served as a mouthpiece
for SDS, and I often wanted Bob to contribute
something. Which he often promised to do. But Bob

10 In the interests of full disclosure: although Bob and I were close friends
during our years in graduate school at Stanford, as of this writing, we have not,
alas, seen each other for a very long time. Still, he is a close friend of my youth,
someone I loved: it would be odd not to call him "Bob."

was a very poor propagandist. If he was going to tell it, he was going to tell it slant.

For example: Jonas Salk's youngest son, Jonathan, was a student in my freshman English class, where—those were the days—we had been exploring the philosophical idea of absolutism, which I asserted was not just an abstract idea but should be understood as an accurate version of reality (if you couldn't draw an absolute distinction between a liberating and an oppressive politics, then . . .). Jonathan was a scientist; the notion of an absolute reality made no sense to him; I couldn't make him see things my way.

So I asked Bob to help me out. He had been to St. Mary's, he had read Euclid in Greek, he had a penchant for philosophy. He knew not just Aquinas but Averroes. We took Jonathan to lunch. My admiring idea of a philosophically sound argument was a neat syllogism, something crystalline, economical, and definitive, a train of thought so compelling that when you arrived finally at its conclusion you simply had to assent. Right. Bob told Jonathan stories, elegant stories that however didn't even pretend to have a beginning, a middle, and an end or anyway not in the sense that creative writing texts draw an arc for narrative, a kind of narrative syllogism in which plot is like the trajectory of, and has the deadly, single-minded purpose of, an expertly shot arrow. No, Bob told Jonathan stories that I have learned from his latest book, the spectacular *Summer Snow*, should be called explaining narratives.

Jonathan was a very polite boy: he never asked me about absolutism again.

Everything we do is explaining the sunrise.
Dying explains it. Making love explains it.

The last plays of Shakespeare explain it.
We're just as ignorant as at the beginning.

We make Stonehenge over and over
Thinking it will do some good to know
where

Or at least when: flame fissuring up
between two stones.
It lifts us as sex arches the body up, it
carries us, up and over,

And no one knows why or when it will
stop,

So everything we do is explaining the
sunrise.

("Cymbeline")

At the beginning, certainly by the time of
his remarkable first book, *Field Guide* (1973!), Bob
had become entranced by the very short form,
the lapidary classical poetry of Japan, Basho and
Kobayashi Issa.

Asked how old he was
the boy in the new kimono
stretched out all five fingers.

These miniatures are the master forms for explaining narratives. Traditional narrative—exposition,
conflict, climax, denouement—contains, implies,
and enacts a certain worldview, by which I mean
a complex of assumptions as well as observations.
The arc of traditional narrative is goal-oriented.
What pleases us in such a narrative is rigor of
purpose, the calculus of emotion, the utilitarian
virtues of plot; you pack your things, head out, and,
most important, arrive somewhere. We think of the
arrival as a conclusion, in both senses of the word.

So: traditional narrative assumes and asserts that meaning inheres in the conclusion we draw from experience. The idea that we can draw a conclusion from experience is at once comforting and, because of its suggestion that meaning is singular, oppressive.

How different the three lines from Kobayashi Issa. I know very little about Japanese poetry, but clearly this is a poetry of occasion, which is to say of evanescence. The moment is intensely observed but is not expected to take the form of an argument. The poem does not ask what happens but rather is transfixed by what is. If what characterizes traditional narrative, after Joyce, is epiphany, a kind of inspired understanding, then what characterizes Kobayashi Issa's poem is joy or maybe it would be better to say wonder, wonder at the elemental circumstances of being. Rendering the boy's pride in being is something like imagining an explanation rather than arriving at a conclusion.

I don't want to overstate these differences, never mind to establish one of those awful comparisons between East and West. What I am calling traditional narrative is also, of course, a way of explaining the sunrise. But for my purposes here I am going to say that traditional narrative is a kind of argument and tends toward conclusion, whereas Basho and Kobayashi Issa are after explanation, the imaginative discovery and rendering of what inheres in the moment.

I heard Bob read the poem about the boy in his new kimono soon after *Field Guide* was published. When he got to the last line he looked up from his book and, with a delighted smile, stretched out all five fingers—as if to say, See! As if we might not quite have got it; and as if it was beyond wonderful, the prideful little boy, on a special day—a name day, a birthday—bursting with the exuberance of the very young at the achievement of ageing.

Nevertheless a moment is not a life, or in any event we may wonder—and Bob usually does wonder—what happened to the boy in the kimono. Which suggests a more discursive or expansive possibility for an explaining narrative, the possibility that Bob has in fact explored, with imaginative audacity, throughout his career.

Toward the end of *Field Guide* Bob placed a sequence of four poems about a pornographer.

The first opens like this:

He has finished a day's work.
Placing his pencil in a marmalade jar
which is colored the soft grey
of a crumbling Chinese wall
in a Sierra meadow, he walks
from his shed into the afternoon
where orioles rise aflame from the orchard.

("The Pornographer")

The question that propels the poem is: What does this man, who keeps his drawing pencils in a marmalade jar, do at the end of a day's work? Bob is curious, wants to answer the question, but not in the form of traditional narrative, and in verse.

This morning the sun rose over the
    garden wall and a rare blue sky
leaped from east to west. Man is altogether
    desire, say the Upanishads.
Worth anything, a blue sky, says Mr. Acker,
    the Shelford gardener.

This is the opening of "Human Wishes," from the volume of the same name published about a decade after *Field Guide*. On the page each line of the poem runs from flush-left to flush-right, so that it is a page long rectangle of type (as is true of many of the poems in *Human Wishes*), one solution, then, to the dilemma of how to render a story in verse. Moreover (because Bob is writing the poem in England?), this also has to do with American speech and the particular pacing of American speech. And, not least, with the place of the poet in the poem.

In a recent review of new books by Chris Nealon and Carolyn Forche (*The New York Review*, May 28, 2020), Elisa Gabbert says directly what we must all be feeling but are usually happy to leave unsaid: that contemporary writing of course gets written from within our cataclysmic contemporary situation. Whether the writer is directly addressing this situation or not, she concludes, "the contemporary poet's only subject is climate change." She incorporates or subsumes race and class in the all-encompassing "climate change," which she characterizes as "the end of the world as we know it." (But then, in the individual life, aren't we always on the brink of "the end of the world as we know it"?)

Field Guide, its title alone a little provocation, can be read as a prescient manifesto for paying attention.

I don't know if "Human Wishes" raises the stakes, but it shows how, for Bob, the everyday sings with implications. It's morning, and since this is England (Great Shelford, just south of Cambridge, according to Wikipedia Britain's twenty-second richest village), the "rare blue sky" is a treat. Mr. Acker, the gardener, especially appreciates it. That morning Bob is reading or remembering something in the Upanishads about desire, which can be a very big word but also, like appetite, and gardening, very matter-of-fact. What is it, desire? Well, on TV, there was a show about chimpanzees using tools, a "carefully stripped willow branch." The chimpanzee purposefully pokes the branch into the anthill to gather the tasty red ants, who pack a fierce bite, and then swoops them expertly into his mouth. The chimpanzee, Bob says, "desired red ants." The chimp desired ants and Bob's wife, Earlene, wanted some old boards for a Welsh dresser. Look at how this is rendered:

There was an empty
    place in the universe where that branch

wasn't and the chimp filled it, as
Earlene, finding no back on an old Welsh
    cupboard she had bought in
Saffron Walden, imagined one there and
    imagined both the cupboard
and the imagined back against a kitchen wall in
    Berkeley, and went into
town looking for a few boards of eighteenth
    -century tongue-in-groove
pine to fill that empty space.

The setting may be a patch of rural England but no English poet could have written that sentence. The commonplace about the great English gardeners—Capability Brown, Vita Sackville-West (Americans rarely get these great names)—is that they cultivated plants and flowers so they appeared "as if" they had not been cultivated at all but had grown wild or, if you prefer, naturally. But, at least in my encounter with it as an American, English gardening, maybe because of the permeating awareness of England as a small island nation, is very precise, careful, and only appears casual and capacious. Also, for many of the writers about the English countryside whom I know—William Cobbett, Thomas Hardy, Raymond Williams—what distinguishes the English countryside is that it is a visibly working environment, a landscape with people in it. Whereas Thoreau went trekking in Maine because the Maine woods were vast and unpeopled; what delighted him was the (doubtless fantastic) idea that no one had stepped in those woods before him since the beginning of time. And have a look at John Muir on the Rockies.

Bob, who introduced me to Robinson Jeffers, a poet I had never heard of when I arrived at Stanford, has lived almost all his life in northern California, with its vast skies and wild coast, and I'd guess that a linguist would find in Bob's voice the sounds of northern California. I met Bob in the fall of 1963. At the time there was still something self-conscious about that part of California in relation to the East, a felt sense of comparison and disquiet and cultural inferiority. Bob says that "in 1941 [Kenneth Rexroth] published the first readable book of poems ever produced by a resident" of San Francisco (*Some Notes on the San Francisco Bay Area As a Culture Region: A Memoir*). But being far from the center in a place with a brand-new culture still in the making can also let you be someone different from the buttoned-down Easterners, or, if you live, as Robinson Jeffers did, at Carmel, to inhabit a landscape whose qualities are so stunningly unlike New England as to suggest, or invite, an entirely different outlook on being human. Bob's acute awareness of and interest in this Californian difference, as a natural terrain, as a historical locale thick with untold stories, has been manifest in his work from the start. This business about voice, then, is as much about American history as about American language.

So for me those broad cadences and long breaths in the passage from "Human Wishes" are the tell-tale signs of Bob's northern Californian English, and especially of how he has managed that speech for his explaining narratives. And please note that it's just these broad cadences and long breaths that allow for the very specific diversion of the slight, pattern delineating pauses Bob uses with wonderful, and characteristic, skill, and that I think are the bedrock of his distinctive voice: " . . . and the chimp filled it, as/Earlene, finding no back to an old Welsh cupboard she had bought in/Saffron Walden, imagined . . ." I can't tell you anything more precise, from a linguistics point of view, about what Bob is doing in these lines, but here is something similar in James Baldwin:

He could be chilling in the pulpit and
indescribably cruel in his personal life

and he was certainly the most bitter man
I have ever met; yet it must be said that
there was something else in him, buried in
him, which lent him his tremendous power
and, even, a rather crushing charm.

The pacing here, from near the beginning of "Notes
of a Native Son," works by deploying those broad
cadences—"He could be chilling . . . and . . . and .
. . ;"— and then, where really it doesn't seem altogether necessary, turning the flow, slightly, to give
the sentence its proper shape as a complete, emotionally inclusive, statement—"something else in
him, buried in him" and especially "tremendous
power and, even, a rather crushing charm."

Earlene goes into town looking for tongue-in-
groove pine but the man in the shop says he doesn't
have any, except that when Earlene, sure she has
seen some, returns, he suddenly finds some.

        Mr. Acker, hearing the
story, explained. You know, he said, a
        lot of fiddling goes on in those
places. The first time you went in, the
        governor was there, the second
time he wasn't, so the chap sold you

some scrap and he's four quid in
pocket. No doubt he's having a good time
     now with his mates in the pub.
Or he might have put it on the horses
     at Newmarket.
                    He might parlay it
into a fortune.

As I understand Bob, he means that we—people or
maybe it should be living creatures—make the world
out of our desires, filling what would otherwise be
an empty universe through imagination.

I am going to skip several decades and turn
to *Summer Snow*, which picks up on that idea but of
course no longer from the vantage point of a young
man stretching his limbs but rather now of someone
on the way out, a man who can say with authority
that he's "just as ignorant as at the beginning."
Which is an important truth but then again is not
altogether true. For one thing, by now Bob has lived
a long time with the elements of his craft.

Elisa Gabbert, when she begins, in her review,
to talk of Carolyn Forche's *In the Lateness of the World*,
briefly invokes the idea of a "poetry of witness,"
which in its aptness and also complexity is so

important to Forche, and also to Bob. At the same time, the idea of witness needs some redefinition, or revision, to say just what Bob is doing in his work.

What is the place of the poet in the poem about the boy in the kimono?

Narrative has two narrative extremes: at one end of the spectrum, there's the omniscient narrator, at the other end the first-person narrator. Arguably, at the extreme, the omniscient narrator is almost invisible; it's almost as if there isn't a narrator, there is simply narrative. Whereas the first-person narrator, at the other extreme, is in-your-face, everything comes to the reader through the person of the narrator. At this extreme, too, the narrator's voice is an inescapable medium, as in *Huckleberry Finn* or *Catcher in the Rye*.

In prose narrative it's easier than in poetry to say that these narrators are not exactly the writer. It may be that we think of *Pride and Prejudice* as being told by Jane Austen, but it's a strange Jane Austen, both like and unlike the spinster living in her brother's mansion and writing at a table in the parlor. And yet it *is* Jane Austen; if you're like me you worry about having your crass sensibility exposed in the presence of Jane Austen, whose presence renders judgment, palpably, in *Pride and Prejudice*. I mean, I want her to think well of me.

The poem about the boy in the kimono begins—"Asked how old he was." I don't know if this is how it goes in Japanese—does it say "When I asked" or is there in Japanese a difference between "When I asked" and "When asked"?—in any event, in English, there's an implicit questioner. Who is asking? Is the poem's "speaker" like an omniscient narrator, and we just see the boy as if there were no speaker, and almost, no writer? In a different vein, can we say that this poem, the one about the boy in the kimono, is a poem of witness? Or does a poem of witness have to be in the first person? And would this first person speaker be the poet in the sense of the person who pays taxes and drinks tea for breakfast?

This batch of questions seems to me crucial for getting at how Bob approaches his work. What is it we are supposed to do, as writers?

All you have to do is say some words.
All you have to do is what the birds
Outside your window are doing in the first
light

Of morning in the middle of July. Like you
They have an eye to open. (All you have to
    do
Is rhyme.) Like you they've slept. (All you
    have to do
Is live in time.) What leaps, what leapt
To mind is the oddness of "July"
And "sleeps," as in the sentence *Every*
    creature sleeps.

("The Archaeology of Plenty")

The poem—it is placed, incidentally, right
after "Cymbeline"— is partly playful (rhyme, time,
mind), sometimes faintly bitter and weary—"All you
have to do . . . ," as if it were that easy, and worse, as
if, in the face of a pointless universe ("the spinning
motion/Of a rock in space in relation to a burning
storm/Of gasses") it makes any difference.   But
more than anything, after many years in the craft,
and too many years of reading literary and linguistic
theory, Bob is burdened here by his gift. Having lived
a life among words, he can't suppress a learned exas-
peration at being stuck with their "oddness" (what is
the relation of "rock" to the rock? but then again,
for us, isn't the rock inextricable from "rock"?), with
their oddness and artificiality, their hopeless separa-

tion from the living thing. But just as the poem gets
to this pass, it breaks off and abruptly takes the form
of a letter:

> Dear A----. Driving into these mountains,
> I had to remind myself that they are not
> sacred beings or the visible emanations of
> some enormous unseen dower . . .

To begin with this letter carries on the half-bitter
play on/with words –

> unseen dower (unless I said they were, if
> you know what I mean), but bare rock
> eroding in the sun. Which led me to think
> that "rock" was an inexplicable invention.
> Which led me to remind myself that
> "invention" was, in this case, a figure of
> speech . . .

until he's had enough of all that:

> I imagine you are watching your girls
> running through the sprinkler just now
> and that's what you should be doing on
> a summer day. You and D— can have

the meaninglessness of the universe, after
you've grilled the chicken and eaten the
chilled melon balls you let the girls scoop
out this afternoon with the melon-ball-
fashioning tool and after they've bathed
and been storied and you've watched their
small mouths make small, even breaths as
they fall asleep . . .

. . . so that the fact of the sun rising every
day seemed less merciless, when I thought
about you two drifting off to sleep after the
movie, hovering between that romantic
imagination of fatality and the practical
immanence that will get you up in the
morning.

This seems a good place to end the poem, but Bob
doesn't, and before talking about why I need to say a
word about how Bob has wound the poems in *Summer
Snow* together. You will have noticed the sunrise in
"The Archaeology of Plenty," echoing? amending?
the sunrise of "Cymbeline." Well, ten pages after
"Archaeology," in a poem titled "A Person Should,"
Bob quotes a sentence he finds, or claims he finds,

in an empty classroom: *"Poetry is sheet lightning/in a summer field."* OK. Here, in full, is the conclusion of "The Archaeology of Plenty":

> All you have to do is say the words. You
> have very little idea
> What the birds think they are doing. Or
> what "think they are doing"
> Means inside a bird. All you have to do is
> say words
> For some imagined others in a world of
> words, a lull of world
> And words that makes a world, or makes
> seeing in the dark
> As sheet lightning does, sometimes, at
> night, in summer fields.
> Or—I was about to write—like rain just
> beginning, like hearing
> On waking, in the leaves, the sound of
> rain. Too painful a way,
> Or pretty, to make a saying or singing of
> all you have to do.

And this really does end the poem.

But despite the apparent effort here to tie up loose ends, there's a radical sense of irresolution in the poem. "Seeing in the dark/ As sheet lightning does" somehow doesn't satisfy Bob: writing the poem, writing poetry may be like "seeing in the dark/As sheet lightning does" or it may be like something altogether different . . . "Or—I was about to write—like rain . . ." What I hear in these alternatives is Bob saying, Hey, there's a person behind the writing, a person putting these words on paper, and since this person "was about to write" the point that I think Bob doesn't want us to evade is that he could just as easily *not* have put these words down, or he could have put other words down . . . all we have, as readers, Bob insists—and all he has as creator— are *these* (arbitrary?) words: that's all of reality we're able to get. (Are these images one just as good as another? Sheet lightning or the sound of rain??)

And one more thing to complicate matters: who is this "I"? Should I see this "I" as my old friend Bob Hass, pure and simple? What is the place of the poet in the poem?

When Bob and I were graduate students, despite John Berryman and Robert Lowell and James Wright and Sylvia Plath and Adrienne Rich, the academic idea, Pound and Eliot's idea, was that all traces of the poet as person should be wiped from the poem—because, properly understood, a poem is "autotelic" (I've only come across this word in print twice: once in T.S. Eliot, making his argument about the nature of poetry; and once in Maggie Nelson's dazzling *The Argonauts*, to explain the relation between mother and infant.) . . . autotelic, that is, self-referring, complete in itself, not pointing to anything beyond itself, no external goal, absent, to pick up another of those words, absent teleology.

Perhaps Eliot wanted to see poetry as autotelic because he and Pound liked the notion that they were reviving not just the classical practice but the classical role of the poet as "maker." To exhibit the person and personality of the maker in the made thing is to vitiate the integrity of the made thing and to destroy the social utility of the maker, which is to say the artist's status as Master.

The idea that a work of art could be autotelic has always seemed to me obviously flawed if not outright ridiculous. But I am not as ready to dismiss the idea that the social role of the artist is as Master. Yes, the word calls up a long-gone order of things, and sounds—is—deeply patriarchal. But nevertheless, if the artist is not a Master, then what *is* the social utility of the artist?

Summer Snow is divided into five sections. The fourth section contains a couple of "notebooks," and one, "The Creech Notebook," recounts Bob's participation in a protest at the Creech Air Force Base in Nevada, a place from which drones are guided to kill people in Afghanistan and Pakistan, drones, you know, that, as Bob tells us, cost $20 million each to build and $30,000 an hour to fly. Bob and his second wife, the poet Brenda Hillman, drive out from Berkeley for the occasion, staying in Bakersfield the first night, where they eat at a Basque restaurant, and at the La Quinta in North Las Vegas the second night. It's Super Bowl Sunday and on the drive they're listening to the game and also to Brenda reading from the *Aeneid*, which she's teaching.

This group of poems, "The Creech Notebook," which it's easy to call a work of witness, brings to mind another kind of poem, a seduction poem, that the Elizabethans were especially fond of. I am thinking of those poems that brazenly wave the lover's mortality in her—and sometimes his—face and then say but, ah, if you go to bed with me I will write it all up and, my dear, you will be immortalized! Aside from admiring the chutzpah of all this, I know that neither the poet nor the lover could possibly have believed such sweet talk, because these very same poets also wrote, with great power, about how time erases all things, and so on. And they didn't have a date, as we do, for when the Sun will run out of gas.

The body of the poet, and alas of the lover, too, will fall to dust, but the poet's words, so the argument goes, can, no, *will* live on. That "on" is wonderfully imprecise, and in its willful imprecision, its complete evasion, ironically, of mortality, wonderfully human. I will die, OK, OK; but not society, not England, not humanity . . . and the delineation, in the human record, of how we were here is the poet's job.

As witness for posterity, which we still imagine as stretching over a very long time—but not just for posterity. One of the things you take away from "The Creech Notebooks" is how delightful a companion Bob is. He follows football and Virgil; he knows about why there were Basques in northern California, and he knows about the old Basque restaurants in San Francisco, and the food in the Basque restaurants—and he knows the names of each of the shrubs along the road, and he notices . . . well, more or less everything, and he knows sending drones to kill men, women, and children in Afghanistan is unspeakable but he is curious nevertheless about the wives of the men who send out the drones and for a little extra cash find work in the Vegas casinos . . .

Who should record for us, who should accompany us to the protest at the gate of the Creech Air Base? Wolf Blitzer? I don't think so. (Wolf Blitzer would be a good name for an English gardener.)

But I don't want to attribute this point of view to Bob, who may not want to argue that he, as poet, is somehow more . . . what? qualified? than Wolf Blitzer to write about, to witness the protest at the air base. But he does want to demonstrate that the protest at the airbase is a subject for poetry, and can *be* poetry, just like anything else. Or I may not be altogether accurate about this: I'm not altogether sure Bob sees the issue this way—but it is the case, in any event, that in American poetry, politics has its own, irritating place. For the most part we don't write political poetry; or we claim, grandly, that everything is political. Or we have a completely different language for political subjects . . . Bob's emphatic distinction is that in his work we don't find separate categories or ways of speaking or focusing in the poems that we might otherwise label "political" than in any of his other poems. There isn't a category—political poetry—in Bob's work. The protest at the air base is part of his life; when he writes about it he brings his whole being to the writing, just as he (obviously) does when he writes about a landscape or a friend's mourning or . . . I don't want to belabor this point, important as, in the terrain of American poetry, it always seems to be.

But "The Creech Notebooks" do point the way to an essential tenet, I believe, in Bob's notion of poetry and of himself as a poet, captured by the "in the World" of Bob's essay "Wallace Stevens in the World. " The phrase refers to how we live with literature, and to how literature lives with us, that is, with the role and function of literature and, by implication, of the writer, in this case Wallace Stevens but also Robert Hass. Bob tells us first about how he understood—but that's not the right word, maybe better would be "experienced"—Stevens, specifically "The Emperor of Ice Cream," when he was nineteen, which requires some telling about who he was and what he was doing and thinking when he was nineteen, and how Stevens' poems fed what he was doing and thinking; and then how he experienced Stevens differently as a graduate student—when we argued about how Stevens' job as an insurance executive came through, or didn't come through, in the sheen of the poems; and then about how he experiences Stevens, how Stevens lives in his, Bob's, life at the time of his writing the essay.

The essay opens Bob's collection *What Light Can Do: Essays on Art, Imagination, and the Natural World* (2012), and stakes a claim for a certain outlook and practice, as "one image of the way poems happen in a life when they are lived with, rather than systematically studied." This mild and modest statement understates the claim, which I would amplify like this: the reader as much as the writer, and the writer as much as the reader is—odd that this needs to be said— a human being in the fullest sense of the word—a body, a body and mind in a certain time and place, a sensibility, a bundle of desires, a bundle of words, understandings, ideas . . . and please fill in what you would like to add here—and this human-being-as-reader encounters the work of literature just as this human-being-as-writer encounters the sunrise . . . with all of their human qualities and faculties, and from within and *for* living.

Although "The Creech Notebooks" show that the idea you might have picked up in school that certain subjects are *not* poetic—say, politics—

although "The Creech Notebooks" show this idea to be plain wrong, it's still the case that finally, if you're going to write from within and for living, you're going to come up against the trickiest parts of living. Bob says of Robinson Jeffers that, "looking out at the Pacific landscape . . . he found himself haunted by the riddles of desire and suffering" and found a way out in "what is not human in the cold salt of the Pacific." Bob too is haunted by the riddles of desire and suffering, and drawn to the nonhuman in the Pacific landscape. But people matter more to Bob than they seem to have mattered to Jeffers. To my knowledge, Jeffers never wanted to write a novel, whereas Bob is irresistibly drawn to people's stories, to what people have done and what has happened to us. How should those stories be told?

"A Person Should," where the line about sheet lightning appears, opens with another line on the same classroom blackboard, Stendhal's famous *The novel is a mirror in the roadway.* The bit about poetry is written underneath the Stendhal by someone else:

> *Poetry is sheet lightning*
> *in a summer field.* Which I took to mean that a
> person should
> be able to name their psychic condition or

make a figure of it
   or see it illuminated out there somewhere
   in the gravid air.

Bob calls these "two orders/of knowledge," and he invokes them to tell us about the suffering of an acquaintance of his, a molecular chemist, whom he finds himself consoling, or rather, trying to console, on two painful occasions, both in a hospital, the first time waiting with her for news about her husband, ill with pancreatic cancer; the second, after her husband has already died, waiting for news of the woman's sister-in-law, also seriously ill.

What is it we are supposed to do, as writers? To hold a mirror up to suffering? To flash an instant's brilliant light on a lived moment?

When I find myself wanting to tell people
   about the lines
on the blackboard, her
   face sometimes involuntarily appears,
the glimpse—more than a glimpse, but
   brief—not exactly
into her loneliness and exhaustion and
   despair, but of her
looking into the pool of it, as if she were

> studying nanocrystals
> or polymers. A vision I seemed to want
>   to conjure
> not to mock but to qualify, to put in its
>   place—though
> the idea is still vivid to me—what I
>   suppose a person should
> be able to do. Sheet lightning. A burst of
>   it. A summer field.
> And the mirror—the seeing what's there,
>   or some of it,
> A light purely reflective, proposing no
>   order in particular.

Well, what *should* a person be able to do? I can hear—I think Bob wants us to hear--somewhere behind this "should" the hectoring prescriptions of a narrowly, puritanically religious old aunt or uncle or priest, and I want to shrug off and reject this way of thinking about our obligations; but the imperative troubles Bob, for there are two insistent moral demands in this formulation, and at heart Bob is a deeply serious, moral writer: the first is that a person should be able to comfort another person who is in pain or need, and it's clear that, on the occasions he reverts to in "A Person Should," Bob hasn't succeeded in doing so, or not as he hoped or would have liked or thought he should have been able to; and the second is that a writer should be able to illuminate what used to be enshrined as "the human condition." And here Bob may be judging himself as more successful, though perhaps he is not so much asserting an answer—a writer should be able to do "this"—as marveling over the very nature of fiction and poetry. The last phrase of the poem is the most assertive, as though Bob in turn is setting down his markers: seeing at least some of what there is to see, Bob insists, is not to take the form of a proposition. The final phrase—"no order in particular" –can be read in two ways: that there is no particular order in the universe; and that the writer should be able to help us see at least some of what's there, but without necessarily "privileging" one order or another, the mirror or the sheet lightning.

So now I think we've come full circle.

If we can oversimplify a little and say that Jeffers was looking for a conclusion to be drawn from experience, Bob seems always to have known that there is no conclusion to be drawn. If there is no conclusion to be drawn, how then can you tell the human story? Why, by means of explaining narratives, which are sort of like a mirror in a roadway, and sort of like sheet lightning.

It's hard for me to get this right.
Everything we do, Bob says, is explaining

But can you explain the sunrise?

Well, no, you can't.

If you can't explain the sunrise—elsewhere Bob calls this "the inexplicable fact of being alive"—then why devote a lifetime—or any time—to mastering the art of explaining it?

I don't know a good answer to this question; or rather, all the answers I do know are not very persuasive. What is persuasive is that I am writing this sentence, and Bob his poems, in the full knowledge that the sunrise is inexplicable. (Imagine I am stretching all five fingers!)

On this grey day what does the morning
say to the afternoon? "Here," it says.
"Here" is what the morning says to the
afternoon.
                                    ("Fog Burning Off")

(And so, old friend, to bed.)

MATTHIAS' LAMENTS

The lament, uttered when love and death are most closely bound, is arguably our most abiding literary form, something like an essential accessory to mortality. It is at the same time the most unsettling, even the most embarrassing form, exposing what we aren't supposed to see. The Athenian audience at the Dionysia festival of 415 BCE didn't award Euripides' searing *The Trojan Women*, the outstanding lament of Greek drama, first prize, and who can be surprised—the play offers no salve for the its endless series of deaths, no tragic resignation, no redemption, no dignified exit. Only lamentation, the wailing arias of Hecuba, Cassandra, Andromache . . . But it is not the first prize play of that Dionysia, by Xenocles (who?), that we are still reading today, because *The Trojan Women* demonstrates beautifully, if that's the word, the particular authority of the lament, which is that it offers solace by rendering grief as art.

In the past several years we have had a remarkable spate of laments, including Naja Marie Aidt's, *When Death Takes Something From You Give It Back: Carl's Book* and most recently Chimamanda Ngosi Adichie's *Notes on Grief. The Fortnightly Review* has just published (10 July 2021) the latest of the poet John Matthias' laments,[11] concerning his wife Diana's Parkinson's and ultimately her death. I propose here a brief account of this writing in the hopes of establishing at least some preliminary evidence for what makes Matthias' laments a major literary achievement.

You should know, to begin, that John Matthias and I, each of us completing our Ph.D.s for Stanford, were housemates, in 1966, in the north London house of Professor Wisdom—yes, Professor Wisdom, John O. Wisdom, Professor of Scientific Method at the LSE, who was at UCLA that year; and it was at a party that fall that we met Diana Adams. Not many months later, in a small church near Diana's family home in Hacheston, Suffolk, Matthias (as I will address him) and Diana married. And then, poof, off they went to South Bend in

---

11 I will be discussing "Complayntes for Doctor Neuro" from *Complayntes for Doctor Neuro & other poems* (Bristol: Shearsman Books, 2016), "Living With a Visionary" (*The New Yorker*, February 1, 2021), and "Some of Her Things" (*The Fortnightly Review*, 10 July 2021).

Indiana—far, far from London—where Matthias took up a position at the University of Notre Dame, serving eventually as co-editor of the *Notre Dame Review.*[12]

So.

Joseph Brodsky, writing about what once were the most famous (and much loved!) laments in English—Thomas Hardy's "Poems 1912-13," on the sudden death of his wife of thirty-eight years, Emma Gifford—says that the unusual metrical diversity of Hardy's twenty-one startling and disturbing poems might be attributed to "the poet's grief searching for an adequate form of expression." But he's not sold on this idea. What he really thinks is that "craftsmanship was a no lesser issue for the poet here than the issue itself."[13] Craftsmanship is an issue because the lament will not do its work for either writer or reader if it is not wholly natural—an

---

12 Matthias has long served as an essential two-way ambassador for the American and British poetic traditions, in particular providing British (and for that matter, international) poets access to the U.S. audience through *The Notre Dame Review* (in 1976 Matthias, too, became a fellow at Clare Hall, Cambridge, a connection he has maintained ever since). His extensive body of work is published by Shearsman Books (Bristol), including three volumes of *Collected Poems* (2011, 2012, 2013).

13 *The Essential Hardy* (Hopewell, New Jersey: The Ecco Press, 1995), 44.

unalloyed confession—and wholly artificial, that is, formally masterful. But the catch, for the writer, is that there is no time left to hazard practice in the discipline: you just have to do it, which is to say you have to trust in muscle memory, as it were, to do the writing.

In the case of Matthias' laments we can see an accelerating stress on his craft from the anguishing trajectory of events, and an astonishing equipoise of response, achieved in part, since none of us hold up well in the face of death, by turning for help to the writing of others. "Complayntes for Doctor Neuro," for example, is accompanied by an explanatory endnote, titled "A Poetics of Parkinson's," where Matthias confides that we should read the cycle as "a kind of dialogue with one of [his] favorite poets, Hilda Morley," one of the Black Mountain poets. Morley's husband, the Modernist composer Stefan Wolpe, suffered like Diana Matthias with Parkinson's and it is her powerful and beautiful poems on his illness and his death—*What Are Winds and What Are Waters* (1983)—that Matthias draws on in "*Complayntes . . .*" The endnote also tells us that "the writing itself was often accompanied by Wolpe CDs—the *String Quartet*, *The Man from Midian*, and the *Sonata for Violin and Piano*," and if you sit down to

read Matthias' laments, you will understand immediately that this music is the ideal accompaniment
for the writing.

Matthias reaches out for Wolpe and Morley
with the first words of his (eleven part) poem:

> Help me, music—
> somehow in the way I know
>
>   that Stefan Wolpe's music
> helped his dear beloved wife
> and, one brief summer, my good friend,
> to live his illness with him for
> a decade,   then endure . . .
>
> I anoint myself. *What Are Winds*
> *And What Are Waters* at my bedside . . .

Morley wrote according to the principles of
"composition by field," following Charles Olson's
ponderous but hugely influential program to
supplant meter and metrical forms by "projective
verse" based on "certain laws . . .of the breath," and
using typography to manifest those "laws" on the
page. Matthias doesn't write projective verse but one
of the great pleasures of his poetry from the outset

has been his gift for very fine, and elegantly paced, phrasing, which he deploys with expert delicacy in "Complayntes" to evoke the pressures, dislocations, and also something of the visions—of distress. The poem cycle contrasts the language and outlook of the physician and the poet, and aims its complaints at the helping industry, as here, writing about exercises recommended for Parkinson's patients:

> Stick your tongue out. Now look mad.
> Now look sad and know the difference between
> Sad and Angry, girl. Make it clear
> Twist and sneer. Tongue it sister if you can
> . . .

Two of the poets most important to Matthias— the great British (Welsh) Modernist David Jones,[14] and John Berryman, Matthias' first writing teacher—will have alerted him to the possibilities of writing in the aftermath of trauma. T.S. Eliot, in his introduction (1961) to the paperback reissue of the Jones' masterpiece *In Parenthesis* (1937), notes that "The work of David Jones has some affinity with that of James Joyce . . . and with the later work of Ezra Pound, and with my own . . . . The lives of all

---

14 See Matthias' *Introducing David Jones* (Faber and Faber, 1980) and *David Jones: Man and Poet* (The National Poetry Foundation, 1980).

of us were altered by [the First World] War." Looked at as the work of writers "altered," as Eliot puts it, by the First World War, Modernist writing can be cast as a registering of, a working through personal and historical PTSD: the language bends, strains, and cracks in the collision with the world-trauma.

Matthias had read John Berryman before he ever came across David Jones, and everything about Berryman and Berryman's work, especially the "Dream Songs," is important to Matthias. Michael Hofman puts it perfectly: "Who knew English could encompass that flux," he says of the "Dream Songs"; "that whinny; those initially baffling, then canny and eventually unforgettable rearrangements of words; that irresistible flow of thoughts and nonthoughts of that degree of informed privateness?" Also: "I love the extremes of courtliness and creatureliness in the Dream Songs" which he observes "vary through every degree of lucidity and opacity"[15] All of which could be said of Matthias. In particular I'd point to the easy mixing of registers, which appears everywhere in Matthias' writing, and the location of the writing, almost always, in the implicit setting of the long tradition of tales and Romance (especially

15 "Introduction," *The Dream Songs* (New York: Farrar, Straus and Giroux, 2014).

important in "Some of Her Things"), with their courtly rituals and diction.

Both Hilda Morley and Matthias most invoke ancient Greek, and to a lesser extent Roman, mythology, because in the Western tradition those tales say all there is to say about Fate, that is, about how to live with what, because we are human, befalls us. This struggle—to come to terms with what has happened—marks every word of Matthias' laments. How is he to do it? In the last poem of the "Complayntes" cycle he does it by reimagining Ovid's account of Baucis and Philemon. Although Ovid, as Matthias says, "can be as cruel in his metamorphoses/As some malign neurologist" his story of the old married couple Baucis and Philemon, poor peasants who are the only people in town to do right by the two disguised strangers Zeus and Hermes, is an unusually "gentle, generous story" (well, gentle and generous to Baucis and Philemon: Zeus kills everyone else in the town and burns it to the ground!). By the time we come to this last poem, Diana has been tormented in any number of ways by what has befallen her, the Parkinson's that steals her sleep, wrenches her limbs, scripts obscenities in her speech, embeds her in illusory worlds of both pain and joy—though worse is yet to come—and so

it is hard-earned by the poet and especially moving
to the reader to come upon the poem's lovely close:

> And I was standing in a marble temple,
> and I
> Was not I. Beside me Serpent Aesculapius
> arose
> In flaming cloak. Diana spoke: *I am a linden
> tree*
> And what I was replied: *I have become an oak.*

"Living With A Visionary" is the poet's account
of his, and Diana's, descent into hell. Her physical
and mental afflictions worsen; what she once could
recognize to be illusory apparitions and visions
overtake her; she cannot be left alone. She does not
sleep and does not eat. Covid strikes. Imprisoned
at home Matthias and Diana sink into an exhaustion and confusion that must have beset, must be
besetting many, many families. Both Diana and
Matthias land in psychiatric wards; because of Covid
they cannot see each other in person. Matthias only
manages his release with the help of a "personal
health-care advocate." Diana meanwhile is whisked
off to a home near her daughter, which, although
doubtless the right place for her, is far from South
End. Matthias can only speak with her by phone.

She contracts Covid, seems to recover, then relapses suddenly, and dies. Matthias never gets to see her.

It is paradoxical, one of the (many) ironic gifts of art that this harrowing story is narrated in Matthias' lucid, sinewy prose, his sturdily American and brilliantly managed English (he comes from a distinguished legal family in Ohio, the state whose language linguists once said embodied Standard American). But it's in "Some of Her Things," a fable in the form of a long prose poem, written shortly after Diana's death, that Matthias most powerfully, and poignantly, deploys his language and his craft. To borrow Michael Hofman's word, it is a courtly threnody for lost time. Brodsky says that the heroine of Hardy's "Poems 1912-13" "is not the wife Emma Hardy but precisely Emma Lavinia Gifford, the bride," and he speculates that this is so because, by the time of her sudden death, the marriage between Hardy and Emma had long been cool if not over. Brodsky may be right, but I think the truth lies elsewhere. Don't our memories—in old age, and after the death of someone we have loved for a lifetime—inescapably hark back to when we, and they, were young? It's falling in love that stirs the heart and memory, not decades of washing the dishes (though there's some great writing about dailiness). Even more, writing about the loss of someone we love can't easily be limited to writing strictly about the loss of a unique person; it tends rather to encompass the circumstance that troubles us all while still living, which is the loss of time itself: *Ou sont les neiges d'antan?*

And so, as I've said, "Some of Her Things" is a courtly threnody for lost time, as though Arnaut Daniel had taken up prose. It recalls Berryman's "Dream Songs" also insofar as its great effort to hold steady, to hold things together, to write subjects after verbs, intermittently breaks down, and a manic or unmoored association kidnaps the writing. Matthias finds he is in the middle of the Saint Joseph River, bound to save just seven things from a huge case containing all of Diana's clothes and favorite objects and memories and qualities of mind and person. Each of the poem's seven sections is devoted to one thing saved. At the outset Diana tells him to *"Do like Henry James"* who apparently had to dispose of Constance Woolson's things after her suicide.[16] Woolson may have been in love with James? "Maybe James knew or maybe not. If it was the case, that is, and the world is everything that is the case." Because Matthias is in the river, and beside him is a giant case, his puns on "the case" (and his play with Wittgenstein) become a kind of meme in the work, an outlet, a permission to howl and bellow. "Punt's a long and narrow craft. Craft has several meanings, several anythings are maybe just in case. In case you wondered, in case you pay attention." In the seventh and last section of the poem, there's a moment of final clarity: "I suppose I stand midstream only in a dream, but I am broken to the point I can't tell . . . I've sent downstream all everything except the seven things I now will list. The case is closed.

The first thing I'll save is your magnolia tree

The next thing I'll save is your
Schrodinger cat called Zeitgeist

---

16 Woolson famously traveled everywhere with a huge array of objects, including:her tear vase, her collection of ferns,a picture of yellow Jasmine (her favorite flower), a weighing machine, a stiletto from Mentone, etchings of Bellosguardo and a red transparent screen used there, a 1760 edition of the poems of Vittoria Colonna, seven old prints bought by [her great-uncle James Fenimore] Cooper in Italy, an engraving of Cooper, a copper warming-pan from Otsego Hall given her by one of Cooper's daughters, Mrs. Phinney, and a photograph of her cherished niece, Clare, which she hung in every room she occupied.

I'll save for you your father's sailing boat

I'll save for you all the wine in Jacob's well

I'll save your grandad's prize: A By
God Authentic Victoria Cross

I'll save your secret whispered in my ear

I'll save this bit of ice right in my heart."

This saving is the work of the lament, waging craft, imagination, song, devotion and heart's ache against loss, or maybe I should just say hope against hope. "Hilda Morley," Matthias writes, "called her Collected Poems *Cloudless at First*, and so it is for most of us. But the heavy weather will come."

III.

This Old Writer:
A Journal of a Plague Year

LOCKDOWN

Cooking, Eating, Writing

It is a cool, clear late afternoon on the north shore of Long Island, a few weeks into the Covid-19 lockdown. A good time to start. The water of the Sound, a little choppy, is a brilliant blue, like the sky, and almost blinding because of the sunshine. But I am inside, and, like half the stricken planet, I am cooking.

As it happens coq au vin, because it is one of the things I most love to eat, and because today out of the blue (sorry) I thought of my friends Geoff and Marie Richman, now, alas, long dead.

My English friends, whom I met in the heady late 1960s, in London, where I was finishing my Ph.D. To pay the rent, I taught composition in the evenings at a U.S. airbase outside Cambridge, but during the days I agitated against the Vietnam

War. Marie and I competed—then, and for years afterward—over who was the better gourmet cook.

New York *Times*, Sunday, April 12, 2020

Of course reading and thinking are important but, my God, food is important too.

—Iris Murdoch, *The Sea, The Sea*

No restaurants? The means of consoling oneself: reading cookbooks.

—Attributed to Charles Baudelaire

What you need to know: Geoff and Marie both were members of the Communist Party during their university years but by the time I met them had angrily turned their backs on all that and had thrown themselves instead into community-based politics. Geoff came from the Jewish working class of Leeds, was the golden boy of his Leeds group of school-mates, graduated from Oxford, worked as a GP in a working class practice. They had three children, two boys and one girl, and lived in a big late-Victorian house in Cricklewood in north London. Marie— about whose family and background she never said a word—had been a nurse, but now took care of house and family.

They were original to the point of eccentricity, always faintly anti-social and of course superior, meticulous, and one of those couples who do everything together. You could not have lunch with Geoff *or* Marie: it had to be both. They did not attend meetings—or anything, for that matter—alone. Geoff was slow, methodical, brilliant, and dreamy. Marie was quick, fervently well-organized, practical. Geoff read everything, had made himself a sculpture studio in the backyard shed, wrote poems, stories, novels, polemics. They gardened together. And Marie was a fabulous cook.

I have to tell you one more thing about them before I get to the cooking and eating. Geoff hated being a physician. He belonged, really, in some Turgenev novel, the country doctor who conducts experiments in his home lab, reads all the journals, paints, keeps bees, and above all loves disputation . . . He said his patients suffered from capitalism, and he could neither soothe them nor cure them. After considerable politicking he landed a visiting appointment as lecturer in medicine and society at a London medical school. What he had dreamed of. But now, as though he had migrated from Turgenev to Dostoevsky, he was wracked by self-doubt: What did he have to say? How could he prepare in time?

In the end he collapsed, mentally and physically, and had to abandon the appointment. Luckily, he was able to return to his practice—and so long as he was occupied, he could manage; but he could not manage the long, empty evenings. Marie developed a regimen to bring him back to health: she scheduled something for them to do every single night. They went out to dinner and usually to the theater literally seven days a week for many, many months.

And eventually Geoff recovered. Now, having frequented every decent restaurant and every theatre and theatre club in London, they would tell you: Oh, don't go there, the seats are awful. Or: Don't go there: the service is rude. Always querulous and particular, they had long ago abandoned following anyone's political lead, and now they just couldn't stand eating at someone else's table, sitting in someone else's chair. From the extreme of going out every night, they abruptly transitioned to never going out at all. And in short order, too, they quarreled with almost all of their friends, saw no one, tended to their garden.

Along the way they got the idea that if, instead of spending money at some fancy restaurant (where, anyway, the waiters would be rude), you spent the same amount on a meal made at home, and invited over some friends—this was when they were still seeing friends—why, that would be much more satisfying. And the wine would be much better.

I only cooked one such meal for them, when I was living—with my first wife Catherine Lamb and our daughter Kelly—in a Twenties row house situated on a bluff above the Thames in Chalkwell, Essex. Geoff and Marie actually drove out from London for the occasion. My grandiose menu: coquilles St. Jacques to begin, coq au vin (! It would have been better to have some beef, but I wanted to taste this dish), and crepes suzette for dessert. A wine to go with each course. I had never cooked any of these but chose them after wandering through Julia Child's *Mastering the Art of French Cooking*, which, to me as a novice trying earnestly to learn to cook, was the perfect, the ideal book.

This was before I had ever read Mary Frances Kennedy (a.k.a. M.F.K. Fisher), but I have read a lot of her by now—and I know she would have found a different way to say "trying earnestly to learn to cook." Because although of course I *was* trying to learn to cook, and earnestly, too, the whole effort, the intensity that I devoted to that evening,

my excitement and anticipation, my pleasure in
the event really weren't about how long something
should simmer—although that's not a trivial matter,
please note—but, as Fisher would say, about how to
live.

I am writing this from home, and all of my
M.F.K. Fisher is in the office, except for some reason
Long Ago in France, published in Simon and Schus-
ter's "Destination Series," edited by the great Jan
Morris (who, in the introduction [1991], calls her,
respectfully, "Mrs. Fisher"). When this book came
out, Fisher was nearing the end of her life (she died
a year later) and what she narrates had, as the title
says, happened long ago, in 1929, in fact, when the
just-married Mrs. Fisher and her husband arrived in
Dijon, where they were to live for three years.

> It was there, I now understand, that I
> started to grow up, to study, to make love,
> to eat and drink, to be me and not what
> I was expected to be. It was there that I
> learned that it is blessed to receive, as well
> as that every human being, no matter how
> base, is worthy of my respect and even my
> envy because he knows something that I

may never be old or wise or kind or tender enough to know.

This plangent tone doesn't have to do with how long ago Fisher had lived in Dijon—it's already there in her first book, *Serve It Forth* (1937)—but rather with trying, though this is a very feeble way to put it, with trying to capture sensuous experience. Or anyway for a person heedless and total in her rush to experience, with an acute awareness of sensation, hardy and also brave emotionally, for whom it is always all or nothing . . . and for those reasons poignantly, even tragically aware that the more intensely felt something might be, the more stunning and beautiful, the more swiftly and thoroughly it will slip behind the black curtain.

> Ay, in the very temple of Delight
> Veil'd Melancholy has her sovran shrine,
> Though seen of none save him whose
> strenuous tongue
> Can burst Joy's grape against his palate
> fine.

John Keats' political circle—let's say to include Leigh Hunt, Byron, Hazlitt—has in common with the New Left of the 60s its unblushing fondness for pleasure; and fondness for pleasure as a political quality, because it tends both in the direction of democracy and aristocracy, is at best irritating to the many varieties of political commissars and consequently more or less absent from most political talk . . . which perfectly suited M.F.K. Fisher, Geoff and Marie, and me.

The central chapter of *Serve It Forth*—"The Standing and the Waiting"—takes Fisher back to Dijon after the end of her first marriage and an absence of six years. More than anything she wants once more to be served by the perfect waiter, "little Charles," at Ribaudot's great restaurant. And as it happens, Charles is still there, remembers her well, and takes that special care of her that made eating at Ribaudot's exceptional (her account of the evening barely mentions what she ate).

What makes Charles perfect? Well, there's what you'd expect: his unmatched grace of movement, his ability to do everything at just the right moment and in just the right way . . . But all of his—for Fisher, considerable—abilities depend on, reflect the fact that, unsurpassed, he knows what's best in the matter of taste, and, as crucial, knows what needs to be done to pull the thing off for a connoisseur.

Cooking and eating, Fisher says, make life "acceptable," which places them among "the human arts."

All of us at my dinner party in Chalkwell came from working class families; we were all the first in our families to go to college; we didn't know bupkus about taste.

But the liberal democratic system of the time had allowed us a seat at the table (!), ostensibly on our merits, and we had got it into our heads that we were going to be connoisseurs.

At the core of each human art is a craft, and the craft involves learning to do exactly what has always been done over and over until you are proficient. Coleridge, in *Biographia Literaria*, speaks affectionately about the demanding schoolmaster who taught him to write . . . by scrupulously imitating the writing of the great (dead) writers. Byron mocked Wordsworth not just for his airy ideas, but because he couldn't manage his meter (but, as Christopher Reid has pointed out to me, Byron got it wrong there).

In no art is doing exactly what has always been done more religiously inflexible than in cooking and serving. The old ways—precisely the old ways—are the best. Mastering the art of French cooking means learning to make dishes exactly as the great French cooks of the past made them.

But the exasperating thing is that mastery of craft is not art. As Keats puts it, the bond between Melancholy and Delight—which is to say, the truth of things—is only visible to "him whose strenuous tongue/Can burst Joy's grape against his palate fine."

Stephen King, in his *On Writing: A Memoir of the Craft,* is very good, and straightforward, on this subject. Forget about the great writers, he says; you can't do anything to become one of them. But the rest of us can learn the craft.

Which is almost true.

I find it hard to explain why certain kinds of craft enthrall some people and not others. At the time of my dinner party, I found following Julia Child step by step glamorous. I wanted to know, too, what the crockery should look like, and the silverware, and the glasses. Whereas I have never found practicing ballet steps or a baseball swing glamorous.

At the beginning of her meal at Ribaudot's Fisher notices Charles' hand shake as he pours, and spills, her aperitif—he's been drinking. She's mortified—though, as the evening goes on, his hand steadies and he redeems himself completely. But as she's about to leave, Ribaudot tells her, "I fired Charles today, just before your first visit [to make a reservation for the evening]. He is on his way to the South by now . . . a fine waiter once, a brave little man always—but what will you do? Everything changes."

The last words of the chapter, after she steps outside into the Burgundian dark, are: "I began to cry."

* * *

Now, about that meal

CALAMITY

My father and I were both born in middle of a world war, I the Second and he the First. And so we both were boys and then young men in eras of exuberance and delight. He was born in a backwater of the creaky, backward-looking Austro-Hungarian Empire but grew up in the up-to-date Czechoslovakia that Woodrow Wilson dreamed up. And I, born in that same backwater, grew up in Manhattan, at the time the vivacious epicenter of human experience, a place, moreover, where you could be forgiven for believing that most things good were Jewish, such as Kosher delis and Broadway musicals.

There the comparison ends.

Because when he was twenty-three my father was called to serve in the Czechoslovak Army and sent to western Bohemia to block the path of the German forces—he looks dashing and martial in his portraits as a soldier—the very first scene of the first act of the calamity that destroyed the world as he had known it. He was an enormously resourceful, genial, indefatigable man. The Great Depression does not seem to have affected his outlook or prospects. But in the years between 1939 and 1947 he lost everything the twentieth century (modernity) had promised him, and at last found himself—and his wife and young child—hunted in the foothills of the Little Carpathian mountains, where he nevertheless assiduously built bunkers and secured enough to eat so that after almost a year in those foothills, when the wild men of the Russian front poured over the horizon, we were safe, hale and hearty. I remember being scared and panicked in those months of hiding, but I do not remember ever being hungry.

After we arrived in the United States and he began to make a little money, my father always kept a thousand dollars in one hundred dollar bills in an envelope in his sock drawer. He owned not one but two tool boxes; his freezer was stocked with enough home-cooked meals to last several weeks. He had a collection of 14-carat gold coins . . . When I was a graduate student at Stanford, my parents toured Europe for the first time after the war—on a "Stanford Mothers" tour. When they stopped in

Geneva, they opened one of those famous Swiss bank accounts and, at Pathek-Phillipe, my father bought himself a stainless steel wind-up watch he wore every day until his death—which I then discovered was worth over $20,000.

I found his husbandry endearing but silly. We lived in New York in the Inwood neighborhood, at the northern tip of the island—a neighborhood of respectable poverty—but a bunch of us gained admission to the city's magnet high schools, graduated from elite colleges and universities, and compared to the record of human life during human history lived charmed lives: we have not been hungry, we have not been bombed . . . I do not own and never have owned any gold coins. What in heaven's name for?

Now, in the spring of the year 2020, in our brave new world, calamity has caught up with me—and even more, with my children and grandchildren, about whose future we can no longer kid ourselves, for there it is for all to see, turned upside-down by the robust precariousness of human life.

How can I protect them?

How stupid I was not to collect gold coins.

NOW
(ON BREAD AND
LONGINUS)

January 2021. Almost a year in quarantine. I am still alive. Although something hard to name though pervasive has occurred to the experience—of being alive—subtle in the sense that there are moments when it hardly seems anything has happened—the birds swirl noisily in the bushes, just as before—and yet absolutely every pulse of light has changed, even when I couldn't say how. Most of all I suffer from a kind of double vision—attached to each bite of pizza, each step, each thought and emotion is the presence of its vanishing and pointlessness.

But I have spent a lifetime paying witness, persuaded it will matter if something is said in the way of reckoning.

So let's start with

Getting Up

After he had stopped writing my old friend Philip Roth began napping. And he was no slouch at it, either. He undressed, got into his pajamas, slipped under the covers—he told me he had learned from his father long ago that a nap was wasted unless done properly. It wasn't a nap if you just closed your eyes. No longer driven to figure out, as he put it, what he "should do with these people," he could take an hour out of the day to settle into blissful coziness. He loved his naps.

"I don't have the energy anymore," he said, explaining why he no longer wrote novels.

But he was extremely sharp to the end, formidable; he devoted himself to studying American history, and was as always a very good student.

So it wasn't about the mind but the body.

If I told him that he was looking good, he would say, "That's not what I see when I look in the mirror."

His last few books were slim, devastating studies of the human animal aging and, now in earnest, though the books suggest this can never truly be done in earnest—of the human animal aging and facing death. The first of these is *Everyman* (2006), the title, as the book jacket informs us, taken from "a classic of English drama whose theme is the summoning of the living to death."

Being summoned to death is our living experience, such as what Philip saw when he looked in the mirror.

The mirror in my bathroom is about fifteen steps from my bed, and I take the trip each morning at about the same time, around 7:00, because I have to walk the dogs. I don't have to travel to work since I am working "remotely"; in fact, I have no reason whatever to get up at any particular hour. But since Fort Greene Park, a few blocks from the apartment to which I have recently moved, allows you to let the dogs off the leash before 9 a.m., well, if we are to get in an hour's walk, we have to get there around 8, and to achieve that I roll out of bed at 7:00.

Here's what I see when I look in the mirror (now!):

I am usually a calm person, imperturbable; I don't worry. But in the last several months I *have* worried, enough to lose quite a lot of weight, so that in the white bathroom light I am an alarmingly thin, feeble-looking old man. I have not been this thin since I was in my twenties—but in my twenties my body, like yours, was solid and upright and I didn't bother to look at it, whereas now, a little stunned, I do look. What I have to claim as my body in the mirror appears fragile and even more hopelessly creased, droopy, and spotted, my skin scrunched up around my nipples or sagging from my arms, black splotches and moles proliferating on my chest and for that matter on my hands and my face, some just ugly but harmless, some, my dermatologist says, "pre-cancerous," and requiring treatment lest they kill me. Running from my right shoulder to my elbow is a faint yellow-green bruise caused by bone rubbing on bone or tendon and doing yet more damage to my already shot rotator cuff. My left rotator cuff is badly torn too, so I can't hold five pounds in either hand at arm's length. And I know that there, beneath the skin and bone, one of the valves of my heart is dangerously enlarged so each time it pumps my blood a little leaks out. That's what got my father, in the end: heart failure. My mother's brothers, both blond Jews, pale, blue-eyed, died of skin cancer. My mother died of colon cancer, but the last time I had a colonoscopy the good-humored doctor told me: "Even if you somehow got colon cancer tomorrow it would grow so slowly that, at your age, something else will kill you first. So, congratulations, this is your last colonoscopy." Further down, along my thighs, the usual spider-web of varicose veins makes a sad frame for the even sadder genitals, about which the less said the better. All in all, however, not bad compared to Philip's protagonist in *Everyman* who is in and out of the hospital, the subject of numerous procedures and operations, a stent here and a stent there. He still goes jogging though and is smitten by a young woman he passes each day—she "had the curvaceous lusciousness of a Varga Girl in the old 1940s magazine illustrations"—smitten enough to stop her and to ask, "'How game are you?'" Which is the same question the famous aging writer asks Alice in Lisa Halliday's debut novel *Asymmetry*, an aging writer modeled, by all accounts, on Philip Roth.

On the talk shows, the answer to "What gets you out of bed in the mornings?" is supposed to be a calling, something you are dying to get to and that you love to do.

But by now I've buried quite a number of people of my parents' generation, including the parents of both my wives as well as my own parents, and also a few close friends from my generation, and none of them, in the end, were bouncing out of bed. Mainly they needed less and less sleep, and found themselves up at the crack of dawn; or more and more sleep, and found themselves in bed at noon.

I get up to walk the dogs.

What I Learned From William Hazlitt

A few years ago I fell into conversation with a man who looked to be pretty much my age at the annual U.S. convention for writers and writing programs, known familiarly as AWP. It turned out he came from the San Francisco area and knew some of my old friends, friends from when I was twenty-five years old. "So," he asked me, "have you learned anything?" "No," I said, "not really"—meaning that what I knew in my twenties is basically what I know now, what I knew, that is, and know, about life. The same, he said, went for him.

OK, maybe that was a bit of convention bragga-docio on both our parts; maybe we should have said that the essence of who we were at twenty-five, the presence in consciousness we would have named at the time as "me," *that* remained unchanged. Because

RECOLLECTIONS. REVERIES. REFLECTIONS

obviously we had learned a lot of things over the years, about a lot of different things, including life.

Also, what my chance acquaintance at AWP and I knew of life at twenty-five, as well as what we had learned up to that point, meant for both of us a lot of reading.

I was twenty-five, for example, when I pulled William Hazlitt's *Political Essays* (1819) off the shelf in the English library, upstairs in the elegant main building, the Wilkins Building, at University College, London, where I had the good fortune to have been sent for the year by Stanford on a Leverhulme Fellowship (the year was 1966!). But when I opened the volume I discovered—as I would discover about many books in that library—that the pages were uncut (You could not remove books from the library, but had to read them there; but you could pull whatever you wanted from the shelves.). I was the first person who had ever wanted to read that book—and for this reason: at that date the English Department of University College didn't believe in teaching "modern" literature, in fact, did not offer anything beyond the eighteenth century. Fortunately, since I was writing a Ph.D. thesis on nineteenth century views of art and the modern novel, the library had a very good collection (mainly unread) of nineteenth century texts. A beadle, in uniform, sat at a small desk just outside the library. I showed him the uncut pages and, without saying a word, he opened the drawer of his little desk and pulled out a long paper-cutter and cut the pages of Hazlitt's *Political Essays*, unread since 1819.

In "My First Acquaintance with Poets," Hazlitt recounts how Coleridge and Wordsworth transformed him from a lost, inarticulate "worm" into the voluble man-of-letters he became, and then adds: "So I have loitered my life away, reading books, looking at pictures, going to plays, hearing, thinking, writing on what pleased me best. I have wanted only one thing to make me happy, but wanting that have wanted everything"—surely, the most heart-rending sentence in English literature.

So this was the first thing I learned from Hazlitt, that love matters most.

Still, it seemed to me a charmed life—"loitering" among books, pictures, thinking and writing on what pleases you.

He was an irascible, impossible man who quarreled with everyone, entered every room scowling, lived on tea and ink, and by himself in cold rooms in small boarding houses. Even the saintly Charles Lamb would lose patience with him.

But when I pulled *Political Essays* from the shelf I didn't know much about him. I did know that just as he, when young, looked with adoring, gaga eyes on Coleridge, so the young John Keats looked on him. How could the man who wrote "The Fight" and "On Gusto" and "My First Acquaintance with Poets" have been anything but a delight, the person you'd want along whether you were hiking across the moors or attending a staging of *Macbeth* or going to catch a prize fight?

When he held a quill in his hand and began to write, he poured wonderful sentences, ideas, turns of phrase onto the page—a great many of them so vigorous and electric we love to read them today, two hundred years later. But his life was a mess. Especially, such as it was, his love life. He so wanted to be loved, he was so vulnerable to fantasies about any woman he thought showed an interest in him. *Liber Amoris*, where he tells in unremitting detail the story of his humiliating courtship, if that's the word, of Sarah his landlord's daughter, an entirely unremarkable but sly and seductive young woman, is a book no writer alive today—when revealing everything

you might be ashamed of in print is commonplace—
a book that no writer alive today would dream of
publishing. No one tells all to expose himself as a
complete fool, gullible and besotted and blind, and
I mean wholly and absolutely blind, to the simplest
facts of sexual encounters.

Hazlitt did.

He wasn't an easy man to love. No one managed
it, really, besides Charles Lamb. And although he
was passionate about more or less everything, clearly
he didn't know how to love another person, except
in print.

What he did know was that without love all the
rest was pointless: what did it matter that he had
lectured about Shakespeare like no one else if no
one—and he meant, no woman—loved him?

Political essays. The literature curriculum I had
been schooled in, meaning not only what I read but
how I read, was almost entirely apolitical. Politics,
if acknowledged at all in the literature classrooms
of the day, was at most mentioned in passing. And
in general, it was as if poems and novels and even
essays had come into existence curiously independent of life, of people living in a certain place and
a certain time, and—well, and *living.* But Hazlitt

quarreled with Coleridge and Wordsworth because they—as he saw it—had betrayed the progressive *political* principles of their youth: it was a *political* quarrel. Even more, there were no demarcation lines in Hazlitt's writing between one thing and another, politics and art, art and boxing, self and subject. His intelligence and sensibility and all he had read and seen, and his principles and prejudices, all of him was thrown into the enterprise of making sense of things, a passion Hazlitt conducted, pot of black tea at hand, through writing.

So *this* was the function of literature. A way— for reader and writer—to find one's way: It must have seemed to me at the time no less than the key to life, and if I did think of it that way what an exhilarating thought it must have been, because I was not then and have not yet become a planner and goal-setter: I had simply plunged headlong into being a twenty-five-year-old "young man" in a time of political turmoil if not revolution, and of sexual and cultural revolution too: so whom could I look to to follow?

All those writers.

Obligation

Maybe walking the dogs isn't the full story. Maybe the dogs are a cover, a cover for and an illustration of my sense of obligation.

Obligation: a debt of gratitude.

The pandemic has forced questions that pre-covid were fundamental but nonetheless maybe abstract or merely speculative, such as what we owe one another, to an uncomfortable prominence: because the question of what we owe one another, and why, has become abruptly urgent, a literal matter of life and death.

And so I have wondered about the things I can't help doing and why I do them. What do I choose? When I look around, what do I see? In this year when we can't do much, what is it, nevertheless, that I do?

Moving to a new neighborhood in a pandemic was disorienting, unnerving, yes, but also nevertheless an adventure of discovery. Where was I? And then, where could I find what I need or want? And most important, what do I need and want? Looking out my window, down on the young couples on Dekalb, with their babies strapped to their chests and their dogs--alert and happy, ears perked up--walking beside them, I am tempted to go there—to the crowded sidewalks, the sidewalk tables where people are eating vegan noodles or steaming burgers in their parkas and woolen hats, to the delivery convoys of UPS trucks, FreshDirect trucks, Pea Pod trucks, to the bright cars blaring rap music, and of course the masks and the garbage . . . But I am going to restrict myself (well, more or less) to eating, in fact to bread.

To get where I want to go, I have to go back a little, to the town of Malacky (pronounced: Malatsky), where I was born in my parents' bed, no doctor or midwife present, in 1941. The town, settled early in the thirteenth century, sits in the foothills of the Small Carpathian Mountains in a part of Slovakia literally known as the Backwoods. Just a hick town, half Catholic, half Jewish, surrounded by farmland. My father grew up in poverty, one of eight kids raised by a single mother. There wasn't much to eat; the delicacies of his youth were broad noodles covered in butter, sugar, and poppy seeds or fruit dumplings or slices of rye bread spread with chicken fat (itself a delicacy). Many decades later, when he had long been absent from the Slovak backwoods but was feeling a little low, he would cook himself some plum dumplings and then devour them slavered with butter, ground walnuts, and sugar. Then he would make a little tea, with a Lipton tea bag, and lean back contentedly in his chair at the kitchen table. He also cooked chicken paprikash with gnocchi, and especially matzo ball soup. If we went to a restaurant, he'd have apple strudel for dessert, if it was available; and if it was a central European restaurant, he'd have palacinky, a form of dessert crepe. My mother didn't like celebrations and so I don't have any memories of fabulous holiday meals. And she didn't like religion either—so no challah on Friday nights. But I remember coming home from school one afternoon when we were living in Quito, Ecuador, to find my parents stretching a piece of dough the entire length of the dining-room table in preparation for making strudel. They had escaped Europe and landed in a very unlikely place, quaint and, according to my father, welcoming and universally friendly, but far, far from home. So, together, they were making strudel.

My oldest daughter, Kelly, gave me for Christmas an external drive of the home movies we had filmed in the early 1970s, when she was all of four and five years old. There are lots and lots of scenes at the dining room table, food being carried in with melodrama, the succulent turkey, the Christmas pudding, a blue haze of the brandy burning along its surface, or a birthday cake, carried gingerly, candles flickering. And there I am, decade after decade, long after the home movies stop, looking intently at the food, bent over the dish as though I were davening, a posture in the presence of food that I learned from Ben Katchor's *The Dairy Restaurant* (Shocken, 2020) has a long Jewish history. Katchor's book, which is among other things a history of the world retold through the lens of eating, and is my candidate for what to read under lockdown, opens with the sentence: "The 'Garden' in Eden is the first private eating place open to the public that's mentioned in the Bible" and goes on to observe that "instead of being a source of original sin, the act of eating was considered by some Hasidim to be the highest form of prayer."

Which makes sense to me.

We needed huge clear-plastic bags to recycle the vast quantities of cardboard and packing paper from our move; we needed to order a new bed for me—the one I originally ordered was too big for the room—and of course sheets, pillow-cases, and a fortune worth's of cleaning products. We needed to get our names on the books of the providers of electricity and gas and of the invisible waves of light that make all of our necessary devices tick. We needed reading material to lull us to sleep. The independent Greenlight Bookstore is not too far, on South Portland and Fulton, so in the fall I bought many books. But it turned out that to feel succored, to feel settled, comfortable, warm, at home we needed the kind of pleasure that comes of eating bread.

But even in hip Fort Greene, with its swarms of "young professionals," finding bread—actual bread—is no simple matter. There are no bakeries.

My great-grandfather on my father's side was a baker. The bakery was located at the street end of the house in Malacky in which my father and his siblings grew up, and already as a young boy my father got up before dawn and, on his bicycle, delivered the day's bread, not only through the town but to the area's farms, too. I don't know much about the bread he delivered, but I do know it was made from a sourdough starter, not yeast, and was likely made of rye flour (in fact, Jewish rye bread!). Now, curiously, whereas for me bread is, to say nothing more (and I will say something more in a minute), a necessity of life, and I love bread, for my father good bread is a pleasure—and he was, for obvious reasons, quite knowledgeable about bread—but not something he ever went to much trouble to make—I don't recall that he ever made bread at home—or to obtain.

So I didn't get it—or not directly—from him.

No, my taste for bread is the product of social mobility: from the moment I first stepped onto the A train at 207th street in Manhattan for the hour's ride to Brooklyn Technical High School many years ago, I left my father's house and entered onto the lifetime I would spend among the eggheads and professors and politicos and literary types who people the cosmopolitan sub-basement of the ruling class. (The sub-basement, because we have no—or precious little—power, even though we like to think of the sub-basement as the foundation of the place.)

I wanted nothing to do with things cosmopolitan when I first landed in New York as a boy. I had had enough of that. On the contrary, I wanted to be stuck in place, to belong, I wanted to become an American boy. Both my parents worked, and I spent most afternoons after coming home from primary school—P.S. 98 Manhattan—alone, and I would feed myself the food television taught me exemplitied America: Bond bread, canned baked beans, and apple pie, all of which I bought—with what money, I can't recall—at the little corner grocery halfway between our house and school (the pie came in little individual portions in a small box—who made these?).

I remain to this day very fond of canned baked beans and also of those little portions of pie, but the bread . . . Still, I loved eating it on those dark afternoons when I would be alone at home, watching Westerns on TV.

But I never did become an American boy.

No amount of Bond Bread could quite remove the alien in me, the ineradicable traces of my origins, the echo of my parents' hard accents when I spoke, the taste of poppy seeds, the dreams in which German soldiers, or my neighbors, were trying to kill me.

And anyway I was called "Igor."

But that isn't at all the whole story. My parents did not read to me when I was a toddler, and I did not read any children's literature, either. But once in the U.S. I somehow got the bug and read *War of the Worlds* and *The Man in the Gray Flannel Suit* and soon enough Virginia Woolf and Camus and Sartre and James Baldwin. And as a young man I lived in London and travelled to Paris.

I recently stumbled upon the late nineteenth century Portuguese novelist Eço de Queiros, whom I had never heard of until a few months ago, and am reading his masterpiece *The Maias* (1888). As the book opens there's some question about whether the Maias, for generations a wealthy family, have fallen on hard times, but the family's steward, Vilaca, assures people that " 'they still have a crust of bread to eat . . . and butter to spread on it too.'"

I loved coming across that sentence. (Or we could go to A.A. Milne: "The King asked/The Queen and/The Queen asked/The Dairymaid,/'Could we have some butter for/The Royal slice of bread?'") Bread, I don't have to tell you, has been a metaphor as much as a staple for a very long time, but in Vilaca's use of bread (as in Milne's) there's more than metaphor: there's a distinct hint of pleasure in the sentence, the pleasure, for an old wealthy family, of eating.

In addition to Hazlitt, I was also reading John Ruskin in the University College English library, including his complaint, in the third volume of

Modern Painters, against use of the word "taste" and for that matter "gusto" in relation to art, because the use of these words implies "that art gives only a pleasure analogous to that derived from eating by the palate." Art was far too serious a matter to be compared in any way to, you know, eating. But on this point T.S. Eliot has it right: culture, he argues, should be understood to refer to "the whole way of life of a people," not just great paintings, books, ideas—Ruskin's "Art"-- but everyday life, the sports people play, what people do on Friday night, and especially (this "especially" is mine, not his) what people eat.

And nowhere is this more true, and true in particular about bread, than in Paris. This isn't exactly news: but you may not have run across the Cornell historian Steven Laurence Kaplan, who as far as I can discover is the authority on French bread (needless to say, the most besotted lovers of French bread are those of us who are not French). He recounts that while working on his definitive *The Bakers of Paris and the Bread Question, 1770-1775* (Duke UP, 1996; 782 pages!), he wandered the city comparing bakeries. "I was enraptured and exalted by good bread. It excited all my senses; it spurred dreams. Delighting body and spirit alike, it inscribed deep traces of beauty and joy, Proustian moments of immobilized time. Good bread was sufficient unto itself, at any time of day . . . *vox panis, vox dei.*"[17]

I had travelled to Paris, on my first visit, from London, and London in the mid-1960s was a dour city, dusty, gray, still marked by the War. If you went to a greengrocer to buy potatoes, there they were, in a dark little room, piled next to the other piles, of carrots and onions. But in the markets in Paris the vegetables were stunning, a colorful, beautifully displayed array, arranged maybe by Renoir. And the bakeries were even more stunning because they not only looked great—in London, only pubs reflected a similar affection for vivid visual comfort—but also, and especially, smelled fabulous. The bread was nothing short of a revelation—who knew bread could taste this good? Just like that, possibilities of living rose up on every street corner that I was simply not aware of as, well, as actual possibilities. Life could be—like *this*?!

And when I returned to London and went out once more to buy potatoes I now knew I was being gypped, cheated out of what Henry James liked to call "the real thing."

---

17 *Good Bread Is Back: A Contemporary History of French Bread, The Way It Is Made, And The People Who Make It* (Durham & London: Duke UP, 2006), 2.

Much the same as I feel today wandering the streets of Brooklyn looking for a crust of bread. That is, "real" bread, something authentic.

We hadn't been in Fort Greene long before we discovered that on Saturdays there is a farmer's market on Cumberland Street, along the entire length of the park, and one of the booths in the market belongs to the She Wolf bakery, who make what a little pretentiously we have come to call artisanal bread. So far, it's the best bread I've been able to find. Clearly these guys are trying to make the real thing, even though the truth is the baguette is no good—the wrong consistency, and tasteless. And it's just a booth, not a shop of the Paul chain. But the batard is sharp, the crust baked hard and tinged black. I buy it, gratefully, every week.

Longinus, On the Sublime

Sitting alone, or venturing out bundled up, mouth and nose covered by a mask, staying away from people, self-conscious about the invisible badge that identifies me as at "high risk" of death should I contract the ever-present yet unseen Corona virus, I sometimes have the illusion that at last I am able to, have been forced to see things clearly. At these moments I want immediately to put it down in words, I want, to pick up another of Henry James' turns of phrase, I want to make you see. But how can I make you see? This is a question, as James certainly knew, about the justification of the whole enterprise of writing, about poetics and rhetoric, and maybe about the ethics of writing—and in the Western tradition the classical authority on these things is Longinus.

About Longinus, amazingly, we know nothing at all, including his name and when and where he lived—but the consensus seems to be that the writing dates from the first century CE and, on account of Longinus's praise of the writer of Genesis, that Longinus might have been a Hellenized Jew living in Rome. (As a Hellenized Jew living in New York, I like that idea.) Longinus' subject is the expression of ecstasy, what it is and how it is conveyed. He wants to distinguish and explain, and claim as paramount, that moment when a piece of writing, for him as for Emily Dickinson, suddenly takes the top of your head off, or, in his words, "tears everything up like a whirlwind." This is the sensation that for him announces greatness, and he encounters it and shows it to us across a generous range of genres, in epic poetry (Homer) and philosophy (Plato) and patriotic oratory (Demosthenes) and love poetry (Sappho) and, surprisingly, in *Genesis*.

So Longinus' ambition is to fashion a definitive defense of sublimity as the product of art, and we get an immediate idea of how he's going to go about this, and almost of what he's going to argue, from his first few words, which are: "My dear Postumius Terentianus." We know as little about Postumius as we do about Longinus, but from Longinus' choice of approach we can see right away just how he thinks about his subject: first of all, by addressing his treatise to his friend Postumius, Longinus confides in us that talk about the sublime is best done among intimates, is not really suited to public discourse, is not for any passer-by; and then, that talk about the sublime will only be appreciated by another member of the elite. There's no point in talking to just anyone on this subject. So although we don't know anything about Postumius' life, we know from Longinus' treatise that he had to have been exceptionally well-read, of a literary bent, of a discriminating temperament. In this way Longinus very carefully selects his audience, and through this act of selection secures his argument: because if we get even a few pages into Longinus' text, regardless of what we may think of his language, his examples, his arguments, we have either been seduced into or have willingly assumed a place among the other members of his set.

And everything Longinus says depends on this literary community, his set or circle, what it knows, what it values, how it approaches what matters, and of course what it argues about.[18] To clarify what I am getting at I want to go back for a minute to Steven Kaplan, because what he says about bread, which is always direct, precise, and eloquent, parallels and crystallizes what Longinus says about writing.[19]

---

18 And we see the exact same strategy used in, say, the first issue of *The Spectator*, where Addison and Steele clue us in to what they propose to do, which is transform an unruly, uncouth class of rich men into a cohesive nation of "gentlemen." They take various approaches to getting this done: they invent a cast of characters to personify *their* circle, they choose the appropriate subjects for discourse, but their great breakthrough is to propose an answer to the question of who can be considered a "gentleman" that is at once radically democratic and at the same time exclusive and aristocratic. Who is a gentleman? Why, whoever reads *The Spectator*. And this ingenious strategy is then followed by magazine after magazine, by the *TLS*, for example, before it appended signatures to its reviews, and by *The New Yorker*, with its revealing signature cover, before it added writers' names to "Talk of the Town." Who was the "we" of "Talk of the Town"? The collective but singular voice of the cultural set comprised by the magazine and its readers.

19 There's no need for me to make a case for the importance of literature, or, with a capital letter, Art. Here's the case Kaplan makes for bread: in addition to being sensuously sublime, bread, he says, "is located at the crossroads between the material and the symbolic"; it "forges complex links between the sacred and the profane, hope and anguish, whole and part, mother and child, prince and subject, producer and consumer, seller and buyer, justice and injustice" (*Good Bread* 5-6).

Like Longinus, Kaplan wants to document sublimity, how (in eating bread!) it can be recognized, and how it is achieved. Judging the quality of bread—and Kaplan is the master rhetorician of bread tasters—is, he tells us, largely a matter of "organoleptic analysis" (a new word for me, organoleptic, wonderfully pedantic and meaning essentially of the senses. Classical rhetoric is built of similar words: polysyndeton, hyperbaton . . .). Just as in reading we're going to pay attention to the words, the images, the visualization, the ideas so in analyzing the quality of bread we're going to pay attention to how it looks, sounds, smells, tastes. But for Kaplan, and in an analogous way for Longinus (and every literary critic who has come after him) there's a vexing flaw in organoleptic analysis, and that is that it's subjective. Kaplan wants something more than a subjective judgment, even if the subjective judgment is the judgment of a connoisseur.

So, how do you get beyond organoleptic analysis in your judgment of bread? Kaplan proposes a whole system, in fact a scoring system that is something like the system used for judging wine and not unlike how Longinus wants to show us greatness in writing though rhetorical rubrics. And if you have the fortitude you can read what Kaplan has to say about grain and sourdough starter and rising and shaping and ovens, just as you can follow Longinus on "Selection and Organization of Material" and "Amplification" and "Phantasia" and "Asyndeton" . . . But in the end Kaplan is more forthright about the whole business than Longinus: "Exceptional bread," he admits, "remains the prerogative of an elite. We may hope that the bakers who experiment endlessly with smells and tastes will bring their colleagues with them along the path to excellence."

In bread as in writing this is the mentality of bounty.

And as long as we're talking about bread, the point is obvious. No one who is hungry is going to quibble about the quality of bread. Also: there are hungry, indeed starving people not simply far away, in Yemen, but just down the street.

I was born in the middle of the Holocaust, and I am writing now in the midst of a pandemic and maybe too at a moment when it seems we might well return to the catastrophes of the first half of the twentieth century. Can I justify scouring the streets for good bread, or the bookstore shelves for something sublime to read?

The young man who spent happy afternoons reading Hazlitt wanted, like him, and Ruskin, and Marx, to turn the world upside down. As if, if you could hold people upside down *en masse*, evil would drop from their trousers' pockets like spare change (in those days, there still was such a thing as pocket change), and a better time would arrive. And so in literature, as in politics, I chose to be on the side of being good: I was going to be a serious man, and live a just and authentic life.

When I finally got to reading Longinus, I discovered that (arguably) it was he who put that idea into my head: "Sublimity," says Longinus, "is the echo of a noble mind." For centuries this sentence has served as the lodestar for those of us liable to the view of a literary life as a higher calling, and so it is responsible for the endurance of a certain— and in my view, admirable— cultural ideal, and at the same time for a lot of mischief in the form of self-deception.

The self-deception comes of the ideal of being good, because the tell-tale signs of goodness, indeed nobility, Longinus obliquely but definitively tells us, are right thinking, right judgment, the *ability* to experience ecstasy in response to literary greatness.

Here's the whole thing in a nutshell in the voice of Ruskin: "What we *like* determines what we *are*, and is a sign of what we are; and to teach taste is inevitably to form character" ("Traffic").

Longinus, and Ruskin, teach taste as an ethical achievement, in the practice of aesthetic discrimination, and, if I can put it this way, in the faith they ask us to share in the nobility of person of the great artists. How does the self-deception come of the ideal of being good? Because we aspire to right thinking, to nobility of person while basking in our membership in Longinus' set, and the latter is, in everyday life, as a social actuality, as an elite, not exactly or (let's be generous) not altogether good.

Dickens knows these entanglements best.

Toward to the end of the first part of *Great Expectations*, Pip's apprenticeship with Joe, a venture he once anticipated happily, has now, after Miss Havisham and Estella have flashed before him a life of different pleasures, become something he's ashamed of. He no longer feels at home in Joe's house; and though ashamed of being ashamed of Joe he can't help it. "The change was made in me," he says; "the thing was done. Well or ill done, excusably or inexcusably, it was done."

Pip writes these words as an adult looking back ruefully at his origins with the melancholy awareness of where his choices have landed him. I don't feel at all melancholy about where my choices have landed me, but I can hardly be the only person who has identified head and heart with Pip at that moment of his transformation.

Because of course I am writing as the person I became long ago, the kid who jumped the fence into Longinus' back yard at the first opportunity.

How do the values, the way of being in the world as a member of Longinus' set, the literary elite, how does this hold up in the face of plague, and even more, in the face of the Holocaust, that is, in extremity?

We have available a searching, in fact searing answer to this question in the exchange between Hans Mayer, who wrote under the name Jean Amery, and Primo Levi on, to use the title of a chapter in Levi's *The Drowned and the Saved*, "The Intellectual in Auschwitz." Amery writes first, in *At The Mind's Limits*, arguing trenchantly that to be an intellectual—"a cultivated man"—in Auschwitz was tantamount to self-destruction, because everything a cultivated man values is shown to be false—profoundly, unbearably, totally and irredeemably false—the very first time this man is struck a random blow by a Kapo. "Beauty: that was an illusion. Knowledge: that turned out to be a game with ideas." Accustomed to treasuring and aspiring to nobility of person, devoted to graciousness, virtuous discourse, to being finicky about everything to do with taste, Amery is shattered by the utter uselessness of all this in the face of "reality," a reality he is crushed to realize he has spent his life denying. He, like all of us in Longinus' set, has masked reality with the games of intellect, and now at a single blow he sees it has all been a self-indulgent, self-deluding game; he is a person utterly incapable of living in reality. He is shattered and lost. How is he to survive when he knows nothing true about living?

The Drowned and the Saved, the last of Levi's remarkable books, is his address, forty years after the fact, of the unfinished business of the Holocaust, including the question of whether, after Auschwitz, anyone would wish to be a cultivated man. To weigh Amery's lucid, brutal analysis, Levi revisits a pivotal incident in *If This is A Man*,[20] his celebrated *first* book, when the messenger of his Kommando,

---

20 In the U.S. the book is titled *Survival in Auschwitz*, see "The Canto of Ulysses."

Pikolo, chooses Levi for the plush task of accompanying him to the kitchens to fetch soup. Suddenly, out of nowhere, a passage from Dante's *Inferno* pops into his head; he stops Pikolo, and begins to recite from memory.

> Think of your breed; for brutish ignorance
> Your mettle was not made; you were made men,
> To follow after knowledge and excellence.

(Inferno, 26.118–20)

This is, for Levi, an ultimate moment of ecstasy, of experiencing the sublime exactly as Longinus defines it: "As if I also was hearing it for the first time," Levi says, "like the blast of a trumpet, like the voice of God. For a moment I forget who I am and where I am."

Pikolo, who is from Alsace and whose language is French (his actual name is Jean), can barely follow but nevertheless "begs [Levi] to repeat it . . . he has received the message, he has felt that it has to do with him, that it has to do with all men who toil, and with us in particular; and that it has to do with us two, who dare to reason of these things with the poles for the soup on our shoulders." Then Levi again quotes Dante but he can't recall the full sequence of verses, and yet now it is almost too late, they're already at the kitchen—he hastily explains to Pikolo that after months at sea, Ulysses and his men catch sight of a mountain rising from the waters when suddenly

> . . . three times round she went in
> roaring smother
> With all the waters; at the fourth the poop
> Rose, and the prow went down, as pleased
> Another.
> (Inferno, 26. 141)

"I keep Pikolo back, it is vitally necessary and urgent that he listen, that he understand this 'as pleased Another' before it is too late; tomorrow he or I might be dead, or we might never see each other again, I must tell him, I must explain to him about the Middle Ages, about the human and so necessary and yet unexpected anachronism, but still more, something gigantic that I myself have only just seen, in a flash of intuition, perhaps the reason for our fate, for our being here today. . . ." These ellipses are Levi's. The next line reads: "We are now in the soup queue, among the sordid, ragged crowd of soup-carriers from other Kommandos."

In *The Drowned and the Saved* Levi tells us he has kept in touch with Jean, they see each other every once in a while, and he has confirmed with Jean that what he wrote in *If This Is A Man* actually happened as he recounted it, that Jean too remembers the incident, this moment that, Levi says, may have saved his life.

I've skipped a few paragraphs from *If This Is A Man*, paragraphs in which Levi discovers, as if for the first time, and tries to convey to Pikolo the sublimity of Dante's wordplay, just as Longinus, or any New Critic might have done. So here we have the whole ethic of Longinus' circle tested under the most fearful, the most dire circumstances.

For Longinus, the ethical distinctions of writing are implicit in each stage of the literary process—in the experience of the writer (noble thoughts), in the translation of experience into composition (sublime use of rhetoric), and in the experience of the reader (ecstasy). He devotes most of his attention to the translation of experience into composition, for he aims to be useful. And so, for example, he wants to distinguish what Homer does in *The Iliad*, which he calls "realism," from what Homer does in *The Odyssey*, which he disparages as "myth." He means by this distinction that we recognize what happens in *The Iliad* as credible—in fact, as powerful, moving, sublime—because it rings true to life: if there were such a man as Achilles he would act as Homer describes, and Homer's description strikes us as such a precise and eloquent observation of life that we are in awe of Achilles. Whereas Cyclops—give me a break. Similarly, he praises "Sappho's treatment of the feelings involved in the madness of being in love. She uses the attendant circumstances and draws on real life at every point." He then quotes a famous passage from her work ("To me he seems a peer of the gods") and concludes: "Lovers experience all this."

So the ethical task of a noble mind is to show things as they are: sublimity, however, comes of an incomparable use of the resources of rhetoric. For Longinus there are two enemies of proper judgment—on the one side are those who confuse "polish" (Longinus' word)—rigid, obligatory adherence to the rules—with sublimity; and on the other are those who maintain you can't achieve sublimity by applying the tools of rhetoric: sublimity is the achievement of genius, and genius is "natural" and can't be learned or taught.

But as we have all learned painfully during the pandemic, you can't just make bread "naturally," even if you're a genius. You have to follow the rules. And—as we also learned—this is easier said than done—to follow the rules so you get a good result in baking, you have to know what you're doing—you have to understand the rules—and to know what you're doing requires study and practice.

This is more less the first thing Longinus insists on in his little treatise, that art cannot be achieved without method. Moreover, "Grandeur is particularly dangerous when left on its own, unaccompanied by knowledge . . . abandoned to mere impulse." And finally—the kind of insight that makes him so memorable—"the very fact that some things in literature depend on nature alone can itself be learned only from art."

Still, in the end, Longinus—and Kaplan and Hazlitt and Ruskin and on to the present—in the end Longinus can only *show* us: What is good bread? *This* loaf. What is a sublime literary passage? *This* one. But as the editor of my copy of Longinus says, "it is not at all clear in what sense some of the passages Longinus commends are sublime at all. But the great thing is that he *does* quote them, and that he is himself pleased by them."[21] We can't always see what's sublime about what Longinus shows us; and, worse, we can never be sure how to tell whether the next piece of writing we read, a piece on which Longinus has not yet commented, is or is not sublime.

We are left to our own subjective responses.

On one of their encounters long after they have left Auschwitz Jean tells Levi that he wasn't at all interested in Dante at the time Levi so passionately recited the cantos of Ulysses. He wasn't at all interested in Dante, but he was interested in Levi. He could see it meant a great deal to Levi, and so it mattered to him, too.

If there is no escape from subjective judgment, can we choose between Amery's and Levi's accounts of the experience of the cultivated person in the *Lager?* Of the value and efficacy of art and those who live by it? But didn't that moment when Levi recited Dante save his life, if not literally then, even more important in this instance, figuratively?

Who is to say? What can we say with any certainty about people in extremity and what

21 *Classical Literary Criticism,* eds. D.A, Russell and Michael Winterbottom. Oxford (2008), xv.

extremity will reveal? How would the person we find loathsome or petty or ridiculously self-important behave in the *Lager*? Or for that matter, how would those we admire or, especially, those we love? I have often wondered how things would have turned out, when the catastrophe struck Malacky, if my father had been the child and I the father. Because my father was an extremely resourceful man, one of those people who can fix anything, a man everyone liked immediately, a man who all his life loved best and was most at home among the men with dirty trousers and pride in their craft. I am very doubtful I would have been anywhere near as resourceful as he, never mind as brave.

But who can say?

Now it's 2021. I have been alive a long time and I have been lucky: I haven't had to find out. What's certain is that the change was made in me long ago, and for better or worse. Picky, picky . . . I feel my skin tingle when I read those passages of Levi's about the cantos from Dante . . .

About ten years after *At The Mind's Limits* Amery wrote *On Suicide: A Discourse on Voluntary Death*, an exceptionally lucid argument for suicide as the ultimate act of freedom for a human being. Two years later, Amery killed himself.

Not long after writing *The Drowned and the Saved* Levi was gripped by a depression that, he said, was worse than anything he had felt in the *Lager*, and he threw himself over the stair railing in the apartment house where he had lived his entire life, and fell to his death.

As for me, I get myself out of bed early on a cold Saturday morning, January 2021, grab the leashes from the hook by the door, and head out, gratefully, to the farmer's market on Cumberland, along the park, to buy bread.

ON BEING A ROOTLESS COSMOPOLITAN

T he most beautiful book I have read during the pandemic is N. Scott Momaday's *Earth Keeper: Reflections on the American Land* (2020). It is a brief book (67 pages) of brief passages, really chants or parables, organized into two sections: "The Dawn" and "The Dusk," a book about origins and endings. Standing at trail's end, Momaday, who is 87, binds his awakening into knowledge as a child and young Kiowa boy and the awakening into language, into story and community of the human group, at dawn; and then, at dusk, he records what we have done, and what in light of what we have done we can pass along to our children, and grandchildren, what against all the odds abides. And so it is a particularly poignant, telling, and authoritative statement of understanding. "When I think about my life and the lives of my ancestors," Momaday writes in the "Author's Note" that opens his book, "I am inevitably led to the conviction that I, and they, *belong* to the American land [his emphasis]. This [book] is a declaration of belonging. And it is an offering to the earth."

The book is a distillation and culmination of all he has written previously, which invariably has been deeply serious, deeply moral, beautiful, and moving.

And yet I cannot at all understand my own life within the worldview, the terms and references, that are so essential to him.

I don't mean, to be absolutely clear, and to use what's maybe a slightly debased terminology, I don't mean I can't relate. On the contrary. What he has to say demands attention. And I remember very clearly, for example, waking one summer night when I was camping outdoors in the Southwest and for a moment feeling not only that I was *in* the sky but *of* the sky, so vast, so close was the luminous star-pocked firmament, so far did it stretch, horizon to horizon, on the land where I was sleeping. The American land.

But I am not of the American land, or of any land. I was not born here, and I did not belong where I *was* born.

I am an Ashkenazi Jew (according to 23andMe a 100% Ashkenazi Jew!). I was born in one of the worst possible places, for a Jew, to be born, at the worst possible moment for a Jew to be born— Slovakia, in 1941. Almost everyone in my family was murdered by members of the ruling Slovak Fascist Party and the Germans. I never knew my grand-parents, or any of my father's seven siblings (my mother's sister also perished but her two brothers survived). There are few traces of those who died: I have a photo of my father's parents, but not of my mother's. I do not know what my father's brothers and sisters looked like. My parents had no letters, or scarves, or any other objects by which to remember those who died. I know very little, in short, about my ancestors or the community into which I was born. That community was divided between Catholics, the majority, and Jews—and although my home town, Malacky, was (is) a very small town where everyone knew everyone, almost all the Catholics wanted, and many tried, to kill me.

Obviously, I, and my mother and father, survived.

Then, after spending just over a half-year in 1946/7 in London, where one of my mother's brothers had settled, my family joined her other brother in Quito, Ecuador, where we lived high in the Andes mountains for five years before emigrating to the United States or, to be accurate, to New York City (because, you know, New York is not America).

I was born in the worst possible place at the worst possible moment for a Jew to be born: but I have lived my life in the best possible time for a Jew to be alive, in the best possible place: New York City in the second half of the Twentieth Century. (When I have lived elsewhere, it has been in other great Western cities—Montreal, Boston, London.) I could so easily have been killed as a small child; I ought not to be alive. More than otherwise, I know and have always known that death is present (but I have lived, as we must, as though there's always tomorrow). Like Momaday, I ask myself today, when that best possible time is at an end: How shall I understand my life?

And when I rummage for an answer, I begin with this: I am a city boy, a rootless cosmopolitan.

Where I stand to orient myself, in other words, is just about as far as possible from where Momaday stands.

Today is the Fourth of July, 2021: at this date, in these United States, Momaday's credo, the lessons, valuations, outlook, practices of his community shame and rebuke mine. "We humans have inflicted terrible wounds upon the earth," he writes. "The arbor is now a ruin, for it came into the hands of uncaring and visionless people." And consequently: "The earth and its inhabitants are in crisis, and at the center is a moral crisis. Man stands to repudiate his humanity."

Our humanity, for Momaday, derives from and is inextricable from a web of living relationships that demands care and invites gratitude. Our humanity is achieved, for Momaday, and achieves meaning, in a singular landscape, through activity and story. He would say, It is good, and it is fecund.

I am writing in Brooklyn, and as it happens Momaday includes Brooklyn in his book: "How many lifeless things are placed each day between us and the living earth? A friend in Brooklyn told me his little son had gone out to watch workmen breaking up a sidewalk. He was fascinated to see earth under the cement. He had never seen it before."

So here I can begin to sketch my trouble with Momaday. For one thing, to make his point he has been, in the passage above, a little disingenuous. Besides, I am a city boy. I love the cement. The cement sidewalk and the asphalt road are perfect examples of human activity, of the essence of what we have done. And this is not just a story of today, or of America. Brooklyn is not that old a place compared say to Athens, or Cairo, or Beijing. One way to look at the cement is how Momaday has presented it. I was a graduate student, like Momaday, at Stanford, and lived on the edge of the enormous campus, in Menlo Park. Across the road from where I lived the lush hills rose easily above the valley. Then one day I noticed bulldozers on the hills, and I witnessed what that boy in Brooklyn witnessed: the laying of concrete on the land. It was shocking, but also illuminating. The hills disappeared, vanished without a trace, and in their stead were roads, sidewalks, driveways, and houses.

I was shocked. However: what are we without roads and houses?

The Parthenon, the Coliseum in Rome, the great squares and edifices of Venice, Prague, Kyoto . . . also were placed on, and cover, the land.

Momaday has perhaps never been in Brooklyn—for in my neighborhood the sidewalks

RECOLLECTIONS, REVERIES, REFLECTIONS

are broken up every few feet by trees, the soil at their roots prominent and quite visible, usually guarded by artful metal railings that my dogs insist on marking with their urine; and the great open spaces of Prospect Park are overrun by little boys (and let's get serious: poking out from every crack and crevice, every blemish in the concrete are dandelions, clover, endless varieties of grasses . . .).

The history Momaday uses for his account of human settlement is a carefully delineated story, and leaves a lot out. And in other hands, his lessons can be turned, have been turned to deadly uses. This Fourth of July, for example, the flag, the American flag, is hard to look at. The flag symbolizing liberty, and associated with the Statue of Liberty, has been appropriated by an enraged, bloodthirsty rabble who have daubed themselves in warpaint, wrapped themselves in the Stars and Stripes, and set off down our main streets chanting "Jews will not replace us." We are afflicted by something like a revolt of Marx's lumpenproletariat and its rural equivalent, intoxicated by vivifying slogans, such as Blood and Soil.

Momaday is extremely careful to insist on land, ancestors, and faith in a way wholly independent of the Western systems of thought that also insist on land, ancestors, and faith. His people, the Kiowa, are a society, or, better, a civilization complete and apart. There is no cosmopolis, no castle or capital to which the Kiowa owe allegiance. The beliefs and practices Momaday draws on are not those of country people as against cityfolk, or farmers as against bankers.

And this is the source of the power of his observations and reflections, and also the root of their limitations.

In "The Dusk" Momaday quotes "a teacher" who was a poet: "Unless we understand the history that produced us," he quotes from that teacher's writings, "we are determined by that history. We may be determined in any event, but the understanding gives us a chance." As it happens, this teacher was also my teacher, Yvor Winters, who brought Momaday to Stanford. Winters had come down with tuberculosis as a young man, and spent some time among Native American communities in New Mexico to recuperate. During those years he developed a lasting admiration for the Native American way of life, and its verbal art. "Consider what is to be seen," Momaday preaches. This was Winters' credo, too.

Winters was a profoundly self-aware American, and a diligent student of American history. But I am not sure how Momaday wants us to understand the sentences he quotes from Winters. Because at issue is precisely the individual's relation to history, which it seems to me can be (oversimplifying, but still) understood in two diametrically opposite ways. One way is, if I understand him, Momaday's way: the individual life, the individual identity draws substance and meaning from place and people; freedom is to be found in belonging to the place, the practices, the wisdom, and the history of the tribe. The other way elevates the individual over the community, observes that we not only enter and depart the world alone but live each moment as autonomous individuals. Freedom is not belonging, but is achieved by exercise of the powers of the self. For Momaday the narratives that recount the national experience of the Kiowa, if I can put it this way, *are* his history, and are liberating. He cannot separate himself from those narratives. But obviously a slight shift in perspective and national history can be a prison, and a deadly prison at that.

And, too, a strand of American history that is essential for my personal narrative is the story of the nation as a nation of immigrants, the principle of diaspora transformed into a radical form of citizenship. What would it mean to say I *belonged* to a land? That I should live as my ancestors taught?

My parents came to the United States precisely to flee that way of thinking; to be free to be themselves, independent of land, ancestors, and faith.

Of all the American books that tell *this* story, the one that does it in a way that speaks most directly both to Momaday's notion of belonging and to our present moment is Philip Roth's *The Human Stain* (2000).[22]

Nathan Zuckerman, living the life of a recluse in a two-room cabin in the Berkshires, is approached by his neighbor, Coleman Silk , the reforming dean of nearby Athena College, to write up the story of his life and career. It turns out that Silk has been the only Jew on the Athena faculty and the only Jewish dean of faculty in the college's history. His reforming days abruptly ended by the departure of the college's president for a bigger job at a more imposing school, Silk returns to faculty after sixteen years out of the classroom as something of an anachronism, and

22 My review of *The Human Stain*, from which I'm borrowing here, appeared originally under the title "Born Again" in *Partisan Review* (2000), and was reprinted in Harold Bloom's Modern Critical Views collection, *Philip Roth* (2003). See page 84.

soon enough his return explodes into scandal when he asks out loud about two students who have never showed up for his classics class—"Do they exist or are they spooks?" The two absent students, it appears, are black; Silk is accused of racism; foe and friend on the faculty wash their hands of him; in the fierce craziness that ensues Silk's wife dies—*They* killed her! Silk rages . . .

Soon we discover that Coleman Silk has a big secret, a secret he has kept from his wife of forty years, from his children, from everyone. The secret is that he is black ("African American" doesn't, in Silk's case, seem quite right). He has passed as a white man from the day he signed up for the Navy in the Second World War. Not only that, but his mother tells him that his family (and his Jersey black community) are "descendants of the Indian from the large Lenape settlement at Indian Fields who married a Swede . . .descendants of the two mulatto brothers brought from the West Indies . . . of the two Dutch sisters come from Holland to become their wives . . . of John Fenwick, an English baronet's son . . . [of Fenwick's daughter], Elizabeth Adams, who married a colored man, Gould . . ."

Silk's mixed up, miscegenated heritage is Roth's audacious assertion of non-belonging as the essential American condition. When I came to the United States as a boy I was taught in civics class that the nation was a "melting pot." People from all over came to the United States, so the argument went, and were dissolved and reconstituted into a new whole, composed individual by individual. Where once identity was almost altogether determined by place of birth, caste, class, religion, race— now it would be determined by the activity of the self. In *The Human Stain*, this narrative includes—as it did not, to begin with—Native Americans and African Americans. In the United States, Roth implies, voicing the patriotism of his late novels, the irreducible fact of existence—that human existence is singular—is enshrined in the political constitution and embraced as the goal of our communal practices.

So that while Silk honors his ancestry, his historical and genetic origins, he refuses to worship that past, to be determined by his ancestry— "To hell with that imprisonment!" he says. Instead he chooses "to pass," chooses the path of radical autonomy that Roth asserts is not only the beauty of life in America, but the essence of being human. Anything else, such as the notion that heritage is identity, is an evasion and a lie—"As though the battle that is each person's singular battle could somehow be abjured, as though voluntarily one could pick up and leave off being one's self, the characteristic, immutable self in whose behalf the battle is undertaken in the first place."

Roth was a master craftsman: his sentences are spectacular, but none more spectacular than this one, remarkable for its clarity and precision of diction, for its elegant pacing, its syntax—a deft order designed for maximum impact—and most of all, its authoritative statement.

Roth's novels show that what he calls "each person's singular battle" is often muddled and made more dangerous by our ties of affection and responsibility to, and our hangups about, family, ethnicity, the works, never mind the hangups of the people around us—all of which Roth has written about trenchantly (and it's a good thing he has a very good sense of humor). But the essence of being a grown-up, Roth seems to say right from the start, lies in accepting and pursuing the radical autonomy that is the ground of the existential "battle" of human being; and the essence of being American, he asserts, lies in hewing to this understanding of freedom, of human possibility.

All of which—needless to say?—is a lot easier said than done. In Roth's work, for example, the "singular battle" is often driven by or should I say beset by desire, which may not be the way most people view their lives; and is an outlook that, let's say, has not always played well. Moreover, it's pretty clear that most of us fear freedom—that is, having to choose, especially in moments of crisis, independent of class, race, ethnicity, religion . . . But all of that does not alter Roth's fundamental point: the battle, even if it terrifies us, even if we want desperately not to wage it, the battle is singular, and can't be abjured.

I don't know whether Momaday would or would not agree. There is for him something of a mystical relation between self and tribe, and especially between self and place, and that mysticism obscures, to say nothing more, the singular battle Roth puts front and center.

Nevertheless it's not easy to work out just what Roth's emphasis on the primacy of self implies for our relation to others—to other individuals, to our community, to "our" people, to "our" nation.

In the 1970s I lived in Central Square, in Cambridge, Massachusetts. Up the street from our house was the local playground, where we took our daughter, all of three years old, to swing on the swings and dig in the sandpit—except the sandpit was more glass shards than sand, the swings hung from rusting metal chains . . . The entire community, all the kids in the entire community, used this playground; and yet it was filthy, unattended, uncared-for, in fact dangerous. I was teaching at UMass/Boston at the time, and one morning a student asked me what in my opinion was the number one problem in the world. Without hesitation I said, "Individualism," and I told the student about the playground up the street from our house. A few years later we moved to England, and stayed for a few months with my wife's parents, who lived in a large Council Estate—we'd call it a project—in Southend-on-Sea, in Essex. The playground across the street from my in-laws' house was immaculate, no litter, no glass. The equipment was ancient, it's true, but the place was assiduously cared-for.

The playground in Southend nicely reflects that community's reverence for the well-being of its members, in particular its children, and is a decent illustration of Momaday's "earth keeper's" credo. The Cambridge playground displayed an alarming, self-destructive individualism, utterly without concern, never mind regard, for the public good, even when it was obvious that "public," in the case of the playground, meant one's own and one's neighbors' little children.

Hector St. John de Crevecoeur, the first to use the melting pot metaphor to describe American life, advertised the country as a place of "fair cities, substantial villages . . . decent houses, good roads, orchards, meadows, and bridges where an hundred years ago all was wild, woody, and uncultivated," a nation created through "self-interest" by a "new man" without crippling obligations to any lord or master or religion, and not subject to any restrictions or limitations on account of origin. His "melting pot" looks amusing in retrospect, composed, in his view, of such diverse peoples as the French and the Germans.

Crevecoeur's farm was in New York State: he ignores both slavery and the people who lived in that wild and woody land a hundred years earlier. He doesn't interrogate the notion of "self-interest." And I don't suppose his portrait of the northern states as a melting pot ever mirrored what really was going on.

But despite his omissions and distortions and wishful (and willful) thinking, I still find Crevecoeur's robust version of America stirring. Because he captures what was and remains the main draw of the United States for those living elsewhere, what the U.S. stood for when I came here as a boy, and what it stands for to all those many thousands of "migrants" and asylum seekers who continue to want to cross our borders: the promise that you don't have to be who you were born or where you were born. You do not have to "belong"—not to the religion you were born into, or the ethnicity you were born into, or the class you were born into, or the family you were born into; you don't have to go into the family business, if there is a business; and you don't have to marry the guy your father says you have to marry . . .

As a young man I was a student of the European nineteenth century, that was my professional specialization as a professor of English. The lives of writers changed dramatically in the eighteenth century—Alexander Pope got rich *selling* his work—but it's in the nineteenth century that the social status of writers, and the cultural role and image of the writer, or more broadly of the artist, assumes its modern form, probably best captured in the idea of the artist as bohemian.

The artist as bohemian is a classless outsider in a society carefully stratified by class, a nonconformist in manner and belief in a fiercely conformist society, a rootless cosmopolitan devoted to art for art's sake in a community that has placed all its faith in materialism (though it never hurt if the bohemian came from money or intellectual aristocracy). It's this potent mix that established the modern authority of the artist, the reason the young wanted (and still want) to imitate the trappings of the artist, to dress in flamboyant defiance of their parents and teachers, to sneak into the opium dens and to fuck whomever. More important, it is this potent mix that established the artist as truth teller for the era of bourgeois nationalism, as the bard of how contemporary life is actually lived every day as against the conformist shibboleths of any reigning priesthood—ethnic, religious, social, political . . .

Today's newspaper reports in every column (I still read the morning print edition) that the era of ebullience which began with the end of the Second World War has come to a nasty end. One symptom of this epochal change is that Fascism is on the march. The world I was born into has returned, yes, to Slovakia but, now, also to these United States. Another symptom of epochal retreat is our withdrawal into our innermost courtyards: we cannot provide any of the things Crevecoeur bragged about—roads, bridges, transport, never mind health care—etc. etc.—because these things require that we pay for them, and we will all be damned if we are going to give any money we don't have to to the (expletive deleted) government. We cannot have an educated and informed populace because the common narrative is lost. Instead, groupthink flourishes. Bolt the gates! If you venture out, say in print, remember where you come from.

* * * *

The common narrative is lost.

* * * *

I recently reread Jonathan Schell's *The Fate of the Earth* (1982), and came across this passage:

> The task we face is to find a means of
> political action that will permit human
> beings to pursue any end for the rest of
> time. . . . [E]xtinction will not wait for us
> to reinvent the world. Evolution was slow
> to produce us, but our extinction will be

swift; it will literally be over before we
know it. . . . Because everything we do and
everything we are is in jeopardy . . . every
person is the right person to act . . .
For nothing underscores our common
humanity as strongly as the peril of extinction does . . . Whatever the eventual
shape of a world that has been reinvented
for the sake of survival, the first, urgent,
immediate step, which requires no deep
thought or long reflection, is for each
person to make known . . .
his desire that the species survive.

Schell is not talking about climate change (as you
may have thought?), but rather making a plea for
nuclear disarmament. But with the end of the
Cold War, extinction by means of nuclear conflict
between the great powers has almost entirely
dropped out of public conversation, out of public
concern, even though the danger of extinction by
means of nuclear conflict remains. Now we are
concerned with extinction as a consequence of
climate change. About this, though, Amitav Ghosh,
in his acclaimed *The Great Derangement: Climate Change
and the Unthinkable* (2017), argues that the full conse-

quence of climate change is beyond our imagina-
tions. The change—in geological eras, as he sees it,
from the Holocene to the Anthropocene—is just too
big, too total for us to grasp: we can put down words
about extinction, as I am doing right now, but we
cannot *imagine* it.

Both Momaday's people and mine have suffered
something close to extinction. These near-extinc-
tions have imposed on the survivors the burden of
telling, and keeping alive the telling, not only of
what happened, but of how what happened should
be understood. And in both cases, those who have
hoped to convey what happened immediately discovered that the facts, the unadorned accounts, as
it were, just could not convey the truth of what had
happened. *That* required imagination—not making
things up, but realizing the full dimensions of facts.

And so I'd say, approaching a conclusion, that
it is as works of imagination, and even more works
about the imagination that Momaday's *Earth Keeper*
and Roth's *The Human Stain* speak to our troubles,
arguably characterized as a crisis of imagination.

Momaday opens his book with a "Prologue":
"Many years ago," it begins, "a young woman came
to the American West in a covered wagon." This

woman appears again at the end of the book, in an "Epilogue," and once in the middle of the book. Momaday tells us he does not know the woman's name, or where she came from. He only knows she came with the dress in which she hoped to marry. She found in the West "a landscape so vast and primitive that she could not comprehend it . . . a world of constant change . . . and, above all, wonder." He ends the Prologue, a mere three short paragraphs, like this: "I must believe that the woman's dreams were realized, that she wore her wedding dress, and that she became one with the spirit of the land. It is a story of belonging."

When he alludes to this woman in the middle of his book, Momaday says: "Once she had a name, but it is forgotten. Once it was known where she is buried, but now no one knows . . . now she is the woman who was buried in a beautiful dress. . . . The earth has taken her in . . . . The earth is a house of stories."

In his brief Epilogue Momaday returns to this woman one more time: "Away to the east there was in the ground a woman in a beautiful doeskin dress. That is all we know about her, but she belongs to us and to the land. In the pervasive silence she sings a song of the earth. Listen." "Listen" is the last word of *Earth Keeper.*

This woman and her beautiful dress appear in other of Momaday's writings, and always we learn the same thing: that no one knows her name or where she's buried . . . and that it's a story of belonging.

I know from his earlier work that when Momaday interprets a Kiowa story he invariably says two things: that he has spent many years thinking about the story, and that he's not sure he has fully plumbed the story.

So I don't feel too bad saying I don't fully understand the story of the woman and her beautiful dress, and even less do I understand why this story in particular is so important to Momaday.

But in the context of my subject here a few things stand out. The woman is not a native of the West, and she might not be a Native American, either. But she came, she settled, she married, she was buried in her symbolic dress, wrapped in beauty and in her dreams, she replenished the earth, and she has fed the imagination, the meaning-making discipline of those who have come after her in the American West.

Momaday's explicit program is to make us observe carefully what is there, but at the same time to alert us to the paradox that we can only observe what is there truly by imagining reality; and finally that to do *that* requires discipline.

And even then meaning comes wrapped in a halo or afterglow of mystery, which introduces Momaday's main conclusion: without mystery there can be no truth.

So Momaday argues, as I read him, that it's imagination which reveals things as they are, and also that it is imagination that gives meaning to things as they are, specifically by projecting the aspirations inherent in reality, the dreams humans want to fulfill knowing they cannot be fulfilled.

This doubtless sounds pretty far from anything Roth might say. Well, let's see.

The Human Stain is the concluding novel of Roth's "American trilogy"—*American Pastoral* (1997), set in the time of the Vietnam War; *I Married a Communist* (1998), set in the time of McCarthyism; and *The Human Stain*, set at the close of the twentieth century, during the Clinton presidency—and as the

RECOLLECTIONS, REVERIES, REFLECTIONS

concluding novel it is also a concluding interroga-
tion of American promise. The results are not good.

As *The Human Stain* progresses, we learn that
about two years after the death of his wife, Silk
begins an affair with Faunia Farley, a woman half
his age and a cleaner at Athena College. The affair
seems immensely satisfying, and important, to each
of them but when the car Silk is driving crashes and
kills them both, the college rumor is that Faunia was
giving him a blow job and . . . (the president, as I've
said, is Bill Clinton). The novel's concluding section,
titled "The Purifying Ritual," is organized around
Faunia's and Coleman's quite separate funerals.
Faunia is buried in a local cemetery "at the very
edge of the dark woods" in a plot purchased by
her female co-workers at a family dairy farm where
she lived and worked part-time. It's a simple affair.
Coleman is buried in the college cemetery. His sons
oversee a redemptive ceremony—as though no
scandal had occurred; one of the sons wears a skull
cap and chants *Yisgadal, v'yiskadash* . . . Both events
are bedeviled by rumor, spite, shame, and—for those
closest to Faunia and Coleman—bafflement. As
Coleman's sister Ernestine asks Zuckerman, "How
could all this happen?" And Zuckerman replies—to

the reader—that he could offer no answer "other than by beginning to write this book."

As a question posed about the second half of the twentieth century, "How could all this happen?" asks not only about Coleman Silk but also about what happened to Neil Klugman, the twenty-something narrator—Jewish, from Newark—of "Good-Bye, Columbus," and about what happened to the narrator of *The Ghost Writer* (1979), that is, the young, ambitious Nathan Zuckerman, each of them prime exhibits of the triumph of the American Dream, men who have enjoyed the full recompense of opportunity, and who are themselves among the American faithful. What happened to the America that enabled them to flourish?

One of the speakers at Coleman's funeral calls him "an American individualist *par excellence,*" who, just for that reason, for being an individualist *par excellence,* has been maligned and traduced by his (fearfully conventional) friends and neighbors, a characterization that nicely fits Zuckerman himself (and for that matter, his creator). When he learns that the lurid rumors about Coleman and Faunia's accident are malicious fantasies, Zuckerman becomes convinced that Faunia's ex, Les Farley, a Viet-vet with PTSD, who upon learning of her affair with Silk has stalked her, threatened the couple, and whom Zuckerman thinks of as "a brute of a being"—Zuckerman is convinced Farley forced Coleman's car off the road, convinced that Farley murdered them.

By this point in the novel Zuckerman is all in, and he can't close the book on Coleman with the purifying burial. "Too much truth," Zuckerman says, "was still concealed." In this last section of the novel, once Coleman and Faunia are dead, the narrative focus subtly shifts from Coleman's story to Zuckerman's meaning-making, his stratagems for reclaiming and piecing into a whole the "truth" about Coleman. Roth enjoys using his narrators, and certainly Zuckerman, to perform the inventions of fiction (if only to tease his readers about our clever meta-criticism). So here Zuckerman is writing a book called *The Human Stain* while at the same time—in the book??—grappling with the mysteries of Coleman's life, and its implications. Zuckerman establishes something like an archive of information about Coleman, for example from stories about the family that Coleman's sister Ernestine tells him, but mainly out of sheer invention or spookery, such as when Zuckerman, hovering over Coleman's open grave, calls up the conversations between Faunia and Coleman that he needs to hear in order to set the record straight. "I waited and I waited for him to speak until at last I heard him asking Faunia what was the worst job she'd ever had. Then I waited again, waited some more, until little by little I picked up the sassy vibrations of that straight-out talk that was hers. And that is how all this began: by my standing alone in a darkening graveyard and entering into professional competition with death."

That word—"professional"—distinguishes Roth from Momaday. Momaday is an earnest man: I have never come across an ironic statement in his work. Roth can be earnest, but his temperament tends, as I don't need to remind anyone, to the ironic, to what's outlandish, wicked, and funny. Momaday says, "I am an elder, and I keep the earth." Zuckerman (speaking for Roth) says he's a professional, meaning his work is writing, he's a master of the craft, an expert, amateurs beware. Momaday speaks without self-consciousness as a Bard—a posture that would seem ridiculous or anyway presumptuous to Zuckerman.

But this is not to say that the competition, for Zuckerman, is not serious, is not in fact literally a matter of life and death. For as he's driving to Jersey at the novel's close to meet Silk's family, especially his brother Walter, who has insisted the family turn its back on Coleman as a selfish traitor to his people, he passes "the dilapidated gray pickup truck with the POW/MIA bumper sticker that, [he is sure, is] Les Farley's," and he stops, and heads into the woods to confront Farley. Clearly no sane person would do this in real life, and even Zuckermana in his fiction has no idea just what he's up to or what he'll do once he encounters Farley—he just treks into the woods, driven by what he calls his "obsessiveness," Zuckerman's word for his creative process or better his professional ethic. And it isn't until he finally comes upon Farley—fishing on a pristine frozen lake, in the middle of nowhere—that it dawns on Zuckerman that he might be in actual, physical danger.

What ensues is ominous but ambiguous: Zuckerman and Farley talk overtly about ice-fishing, the repose of being alone in the unmolested wilderness, and God, while actually talking about Faunia and Coleman and murder. Roth brilliantly depicts a scene of implicit violence, increasingly tense and threatening, which nevertheless never once involves an overt threatening word or act. Zuckerman gets out alive, gets to write his book, which he ends like this: "Only rarely, at the end of our century, does life offer up a vision as pure and peaceful as this one: a solitary man on a bucket, fishing through eighteen inches of ice in a lake that's constantly turning over its water atop an arcadian mountain in America." The final irony.

Zuckerman finishes the book but does not end the story: "there really is no bottom to what is not known," he says. "The truth about us is endless. As are the lies." We don't learn what Walter tells Zuckerman. Nor can we know how Coleman Silk saw himself, in the end. Zuckerman admires him, but Roth destroys him. A Classicist, a Humanist, Silk is brought down by the heirs of Humanism— the proponents of racial justice, of equality between the sexes, of sexual liberation. If Silk is an American individualist *par excellence*, then, according to Roth in *The Human Stain*, something vicious and self-destructive has overtaken the culture, a universal *ressentiment* afflicting the grunts as much as the universities.

But if Coleman Silk is destroyed, what about Zuckerman? And what about Zuckerman's book?

When I lived in London in the 70s I was a patient for a time of an Irish psychotherapist with an office near Anna Freud's house. He was a man with a very dry sense of humor. His invariable answer to my obligatory, "How are you?" was, "It's a struggle," a sentence he spoke, for good measure, in a sonorous bass with a thick Irish accent, a kind of Gaelic version of Freud's Viennese German. His point—like Zuckerman's, and Roth's—was that the singular battle not only can't be abjured, but has to be waged each day, and has no conclusion (even after death, Coleman's story does not have an ending), and the better we recognize these to be the facts the better our chances of getting through the day with some grace. From this perspective *The Human Stain* looks like a primer in the uses of the imagination, and Zuckerman's "obsessiveness" as an apt and daring form of sustained moral meditation, especially apt at a historical moment bereft of decency and public ideals.

I don't know if we can resuscitate, or re-imagine the common narrative, which bound together the individual's singular battle and the communal ideal. In *The Human Stain*, through Coleman and Faunia's relationship, Roth delicately, I am tempted to say sweetly shows the purpose of the singular battle, if I can put it this way, to be the affirmation or realization of being, of being pure and simple, the Humanist's "goal" for the examined life. And if that seems paradoxically unintellectual, and sounds like not much, I'd argue it's no more paradoxical than, as Montaigne says, that you need a good deal of knowledge and in particular self-knowledge to understand that you don't know anything.

It's a struggle.

ANOTHER SUMMER

The famous Tu Fu called himself humble.
   Maybe he was.
In his river village, it was summer. Slow,
The swallows coming and going as they
    pleased.
Charles Wright, reading Tu Fu in the summer,
Saw darkness ahead. Two old men,
And me too. Another summer. In the farmer's
   market,
There are radishes, chives, kohlrabi, and
Delicious summer fruit. The plums are
   especially good,
And the apricots. And the tomatoes, plump,
   vermillion.
Out of the corner of my eye I catch a glimpse,
At the back of the booths, among the black
   lettuce leaves
dropped in the gutter, of the agile little sparrows,
and the blackbirds, and the fat, indomitable rats.

ABOUT THE AUTHOR

Igor Webb was born in Slovakia and raised in the Inwood section of Manhattan. His poetry, fiction, and essays have appeared in, among other places, *The New Yorker, Partisan Review, The Hudson Review, The American Scholar, The Fortnightly Review* and *Notre Dame Review*. He is Professor of English at Adelphi University. Among his other books are *Christopher Smart's Cat* (Dos Madress Press, 2018), *Rereading the Nineteenth Century* (Palgrave Macmillan, 2010) and the memoir *Against Capitulation* (Quartet Books, 1984).

Made in the USA
Middletown, DE
12 May 2022